MARITIME SOUTHAMPTON

SOUTHAMPTON
CITY COUNCIL

MARITIME SOUTHAMPTON

Alastair Arnott

breedon **books**
PUBLISHING

First published in Great Britain in 2002 by
The Breedon Books Publishing Company Limited
Breedon House, 3 The Parker Centre,
Derby, DE21 4SZ.

ISBN 1 85983 297 0

Printed and bound by Butler & Tanner, Frome, Somerset, England.
Cover printing by Lawrence-Allen Colour Printers, Weston-super-Mare, Somerset.

Contents

Acknowledgements

Many people have contributed to this book. I would particularly like to thank Councillor Burke for setting the scene and Bert Moody and Alan Jones for their expert guidance and advice. Modern photographic printing and copying, where required, has been done by John Lawrence and Chris Webb in almost equal measure.

The collections of Cultural Services contain many unique images of the maritime history of Southampton and I have drawn heavily on the material from Phillips, Associated British Ports Plc, Kennaway, Cozens, Harland & Wolff, Scott-Paine, Bealing, Hallett-Gerrard, Borrough-Hill, Szlumper and other collections.

Others who have allowed material to be reproduced include Costain Ltd, Lt Col Franklin, Hampshire Fire and Rescue Service, Furness, Withy Ltd, Mrs Butler, the *Southern Daily Echo*, Mme Chazallet, Miss Cozens, Mrs Handley, Red Funnel Group, Vosper Thornycroft Ltd, Esso Petroleum Co Ltd, and Southampton Container Port.

I am particularly grateful to Picsales.com for permission to use contemporary material relating to the Docks and Southampton Container Port, for this has enabled the story to be brought up to date.

Every care has been taken to ensure that no illustration has been used without consent; however all attempts to trace parties having connection to the cover illustration have failed.

As well as capturing important moments in the maritime life of Southampton in his drawings and watercolours, Arthur Cozens collected many notes and cuttings relating to Southampton and these have proved an invaluable source of information.

Foreword

I AM pleased and proud to write the foreword for this very important publication.

The importance of our port to this city and region cannot be underestimated, not only in employment and economic terms, but also in focusing the eyes of the world on Southampton.

The history of the port goes back in the mists of time; indeed, it is the reason for the city's existence. Not only has it been the starting and finishing point for many historic voyages, it was indeed also the first 'airport' in its true sense. Great liners and great aircraft have used the sea to transport vast numbers of people to every corner of the world.

From troops bound for the battle of Agincourt to passengers on the *Titanic*, from Schneider Trophy winners to Battle of Britain victors in their Spitfires, all have used the Solent as their pathway into history.

In the mid-20th century, local people were able to take advantage of the 'Silver City' aircraft that transported passengers and their cars across to Europe, following the blade of sparkling water that leads us to the sea.

As a port employee who has always worked at Southampton, I have seen tremendous changes in the type and size of ships and in the cargoes they carry: cars, fruit, people, containers, oil, timber – the hallmark of a truly versatile port.

Alongside the activity of the commercial dock is the vast number of people who use the Solent for recreation. All manner of size and type of yachts and other vessels are present here, from Volvo Ocean racers to dinghies sailed by beginners, from *Disney Magic* to *QE3*, and from *Canberra* to *Oriana*.

This unique port, with its constant high waters and deep-water berths, has served the city well. It is now preparing to serve for the next millennium, with investment, redevelopment and innovation to provide the very best needed to remain at the forefront of Britain's transport industry.

We are an island, and our ports are vital to our continued growth and well-being. We still use them for 60 per cent of our trade.

This port and those who work there are ready and prepared to retain and enhance Southampton's status as 'Gateway to the World'.

Councillor Derek Burke, JP
Cabinet Member for the Leisure
and Tourism Portfolio

Introduction

THE true significance of Southampton lies in the unique combination of the situation of the town at the head of Southampton Water, allied with the character of its people. Quick to take advantage of new innovations, they have developed the port in response to changes in merchant ship design, resulting in the world class maritime terminal that is today's Southampton.

This book draws almost exclusively on the rich and diverse resources of Southampton City Cultural Services for its material, much of which will not have been seen before. The images record the events large and small which go to make up the picture of a vibrant port at the heart of a community that, through the ages, has played an important part in world events. Sometimes, as during wartime, the port and its people have helped to change history, at others the work has gone steadily on, providing a secure foundation for the trade on which the prosperity of the nation depends.

What is shown here is inevitably a partial view because it is dependent on what has survived, and of that, what people have chosen to make available. Sometimes, as with photographs of dock activity during World War One, the material seems not to exist; in other cases, novelty has been the deciding factor.

This book may seem to be a catalogue of superlatives. No doubt it is. At one time, the largest passenger ships in the world used the port, and because of the relative insignificance of cargo ships, these great liners were the largest ships of any sort. They were also the fastest, because rapid communication was important.

Types of cargo have changed over the years and the volume handled has increased several fold. These are evolutionary changes. The revolutionary change came with the container.

Invented during the 19th century, it took many years for their use to become widespread, because docks in both the sending and receiving countries have to have the equipment to handle them. The crucial thing is that the job of the shipper no longer ends when the goods are deposited on the quayside. Containers have to be delivered to a specific customer, and then returned and reused, so there is less handling and storage of goods at the docks and complicated loading plans for the holds are a thing of the past. As a result, fewer people are employed in the loading and unloading of vessels, so relative to the volume of goods handled there are far fewer people engaged in dock work now than half a century ago.

The passenger ship as a means of communication is virtually a thing of the past and were it not for occasional scheduled crossings of the Atlantic by *Queen Elizabeth 2*, would have ceased completely. The cruise ship has replaced the liner, but the standards of elegance and comfort remain the same and the number of passengers has increased to almost rival that of the golden age of travel during the 1930s.

The Southern Railway was reluctant to construct the dry dock at the Millbrook end of the Western Dock because it thought it would be little used. However it remains a great asset to the port, although the five hundred-year tradition of shipbuilding seems set to be broken.

The use of privately owned pleasure craft has added another dimension to the port with the development of housing, marina and leisure facilities on the older part of the waterfront near the town centre.

A time line of the major events has been included to assist readers in understanding the development of the port.

SOUTHAMPTON DOCKS

Some Key Dates

Monarchs (left margin): George III · Geo.IV · Wm.IV · Victoria

Organisations (margins): Southampton Dock Company · London & South Western Railway

Wars (margins): Crimean War · Zulu War · Boer War · World War One · Edward VI

1808	Reconstitution of the Harbour Board
1815	First steam ship visits south coast
1820	First steamship based in Southampton (*Prince of Coburg*)
1833	First Royal Pier opened by Princess Victoria
1836	Floating bridge to Woolston inaugurated
1836	Dock foundation meeting Foundation stone laid by Admiral Sir Lucius Curtis
1840	Royal Southern Yacht Club founded
1840	Railway to London completed as London and Southampton Railway (later London and South Western Railway) Peninsular & Oriental Steam Navigation Co. start using dock
1842	Royal Mail Steam Packet Co. start using the dock
1843	*Tartar* brig explosion
1845	Regular cross-channel steamers begin service
1846	First dry dock opened
1851	1st Americas Cup Race
1851	Inner Dock opened/Refuge Buoy Beacon installed at Calshot Spit.
1853	Crimean War
1857	Union Steam Ship Co. begins South African service
1858	Entrance to inner dock widened and deepened
1860	Southampton, IoW & South of England Royal Mail Steam Packet Co. formed
1862	LSWR takes over the operation of the channel ferries
1867	Imperial Hotel
1873	Construction of Itchen quay started (completed in 3 years)
1874	P & O begin diverting their traffic to London
1876	Itchen Quays opened
1879	Zulu War
1879	Fourth dry dock completed (mostly for Union Line)
1890	Empress Dock opened
1892	LSWR takes over dock company
1892	New Royal Pier opened by Duke of Connaught
1893	American Line moves to Southampton
1894	Southampton designated 'Principal Military Port of Great Britain'
1895	Prince of Wales Dry Dock opened.
1899	Boer War
1900	Union Castle line formed
1901	South Quay and Test Quays opened/International Cold Store and Ice Co. founded
1905	Trafalgar Dry Dock opened
1907	White Star Line moves some services to Southampton
1911	Ocean Dock completed
1912	*Titanic* sails
1913	Formation of Southampton Harbour Board
1914	World War One. Docks taken over by Government (No.1 Military Embarkation Port)
1919	Cunard Line, Canadian Pacific Steam Ship Co. and Alexandra Towing Co move to Southampton
1920	Atlantic, Gulf and West Indies Steam Ship Co. begin refinery
1923	Southern Railway formed Parliamentary approval for Western Docks
1923	British Marine Air Navigation flies to Channel Islands
1924	Floating Dry Dock arrives

Timeline labels (left margin): George V | Southern Railway | George VI | British Transport Commission | World War Two | Korean War

1925 P & O returns regular services to Southampton

1929 British Marine Air Navigation end operations

1932 First liner berths at Western Docks

1933 King George V Graving Dock opened

1935 French Line starts calling at Southampton

1935 Additional rail lines between Southampton and Millbrook laid with connection to New Dock for boat trains

1937 Flying boat services commence

1938 Docks Centenary. Southampton becomes Empire Air Base.

1939 World War Two. Regular civilian services cease

1940-1 Air raids

1942 14th Major Port

1948 Marine Air Terminal

1948 Nationalisation of docks Formation of BTC

1949 Passenger services return to normal

1950 Ocean Terminal opened

1952 Esso Oil Terminal opened at Fawley

1954 STC cable factory opens

1956 First Tall Ships Race (won by Warsash School of Navigation)

1956 Union Castle Terminal opened

1958 Port operations and information service opened (at Calshot)

1958 Marine Air Terminal closed

1962 End of troop transport by sea

1963 British Transport Docks Board takes over running of dock

1964 Railway steamers end service

1964 Filling in of Inner Dock

1965 De-casualisation of Dock labour

1965 Ro-Ro terminal opened for Thoresen, Normandy Ferries and Swedish Lloyd

1967 Modified Outer dock renamed Princess Alexandra Dock

Timeline labels (right margin): Elizabeth II | British Transport Docks Board | Associated British Ports Plc | Falklands War | Gulf War

1968 First quays of Container Terminal opened

1969 Harbour Board and BTDB amalgamate

1969 International Boat Show inaugurated

1972 110 berth Ro-Ro terminal opened

1977 Floating Bridge replaced by Woolston Bridge

1979 Prince Charles Container port opened

1980 Closure of Ocean Terminal

1982 ABP formed to take over docks

1982 Falklands War (April – July)

1982 47 Berth Grain Silos fully operational

1983 Ocean Terminal demolished

1983 36 Berth Grain Silos opened

1984 Freeport formed

1984 Princess Alexandra Dock (formerly Outer Dock) redeveloped as Ocean Village

1988 150th Anniversary

1991 'Ocean Gate' new office for ABP opened near 45 Berth.

1991 Canary Fruit and Vegetable Terminal opened at 104 Berth.

1992 Windward Terminal opened for Geest banana traffic.

1996 University Oceanography Centre opened at Empress Dock.

1997 Additional container berths opened and container cranes erected.

2000 UK Premier Cruise Port (165 cruise ships called)

2000 The Container Terminal handled 1,000,000 TEU for the first time.

2003 Mayflower Terminal due to open.

The Waterfront

IN 1888 a canoe, which had been hollowed out by burning and has every appearance of ancient origin, was found in mud in the River Hamble, giving credence to the belief that prehistoric inhabitants had used the waterside. The discovery in 2000, by the City's Archaeology Unit, of wooden posts originally forming a jetty, gives further evidence of the long-standing links binding Southampton to the sea. Initial dating suggests that these posts were installed during the Roman period, so in spite of the lack of written records it may be that the Roman port of Clausentum could even have rivalled Dover in importance.

From archaeological evidence, there is no doubt that Southampton was one of the most important towns in northern Europe, being the focus of trade by sea with other nations. This activity continued through the mediaeval period when both the north European cog and the southern galley were to be seen in these waters. The form of the old part of the town evolved at this time, and the street names are a lasting reminder of the importance of international trade to the population.

A visit to the Archaeology Museum at God's House Tower is recommended for those interested in the history of mediaeval Southampton. The Port Books in the City Archives identify some of the activities in the port from at least the 15th century.

Most of the waterfront area covered in this book can be seen and understood by examining the first two illustrations.

The first shows the original area developed for shipping from 1838 and extends southward from the old town. The River Test flows along the top of the picture to meet the River Itchen, which flows along the bottom edge and the confluence of the two forms Southampton Water. With Marchwood on the far bank, this continues leftwards towards Hythe and Fawley and Netley on the near bank until one reaches the extent of the former Harbour Board at Calshot. Progressing up the Itchen to the lower right, Woolston is on the near bank and Northam on the opposite side.

Only three of the original group of docks are shown, so the probable date is 1890 as the Itchen quays are already developed, but the Prince of Wales Dry Dock has not been built. Towards the centre is the first or Outer Dock, with the closed or Inner Dock leading from this, and towards the left, the newly established Empress Dock. The final developments not shown were the creation of the Trafalgar Dry Dock and White Star, later Ocean Dock on the further edge of Empress Dock. The location of the New or Western Docks is out of view in the top right.

The other view dates from 1971 and is looking west from Mayflower Park which is just out of view in the bottom right hand corner. Continuing up from this is the long quay of the New or Western Docks, with the King George V Graving Dock at an angle in the corner. To the right is the filled-in bay of the Western Shore. In the far distance a rectangular area can be seen in process of reclamation.

This had the original container berths on the face presented to the viewer. The new container berths going off into the distance towards Redbridge are in process of formation. The gasholder marks the site of Millbrook with its maritime freightliner terminal. On the left or southern bank of the Test can be seen a now disused power station with Husbands Shipyard and jetty projecting towards the centre of the picture. Beneath this and almost out of view in the bottom left, is Marchwood Military Port, with Hythe Marina beyond that. Further east, also in Hythe, stood the factory of the British Power Boat Company.

Sandwiched between these two principal dock areas, on the Southampton side, is the Town Quay. Based on ancient foundations, it was extended several times and now serves for business and recreation. Red Funnel Ferries to the Isle of Wight depart from here. To the west of Town Quay lies the Royal Pier, no longer in use. The first pier on this location was constructed in 1833, and pioneered the use of this part of the waterfront for leisure and pleasure. P & O vessels on the Alexandria service departed from the pier before the Suez Canal was completed in 1869.

The original area developed for shipping from 1838, extending southwards from the old town. (*SCC*)

A view looking west from Mayflower Park in 1971. (*ABP/484*)

The new Inner Dock, open to traffic but as yet unfinished, as depicted in the *Illustrated London News* in January 1852. The view is looking towards the entrance lock with the completed quay walls ahead and to the left. Construction to this stage was said to have taken the remarkably short time of eight months. *(ILN)*

Captain George Peacock not only made an important contribution to the development of the modern navigation buoy, he was also superintendent and dock master of the Southampton Dock Company from 1852 to 1854. His inventive mind led him to develop anti-fouling paint at this time. *(SCC/774.1983)*

The rich diversity of buildings in Canute Road owes much to the dominant shipping companies, all of which established offices near the docks. The offices of the Royal Mail Steam Packet Company were near the railway station in Terminus Terrace, seen here in the early 20th century. (*Furness, Withy*)

Looking into the Empress Dock from the river entrance in about 1920 with ships of the Royal Mail and Union Castle lines. The Dock was opened by Queen Victoria on 26 July 1890. The Prince of Wales Dry Dock of 1895 is just out of view to the left. The four funnels of the *Olympic* are visible in the Ocean Dock. (*SCC/M2419*)

Ceremonial laying of the first 'monolith block' in 1929. These pre-cast concrete sections formed the water-side edge of the New (later Western) Docks. (*ABP/1695*)

Two views in opposite directions from what became Mayflower Park, both taken in the early 1930s. The park is the contractor's base with materials, industrial locomotives and construction plant. The view looking west shows the new pump house and the developing quay wall, dredging equipment, and water still to the landward side. (*ABP/1729*)

The other view, looking east, shows much of the existing waterfront unaffected by the work. There are three pleasure steamers at the pier (*Queen, Bournemouth Queen* and *Solent Queen*). The Town Quay is relatively quiet, the floating dry dock is empty, while the *Mauretania* is in the Trafalgar Dry Dock and the *Majestic* is in the Ocean Dock. (*ABP/1822*)

This view of the Western Docks in 1935 shows the completed and fully functioning line of quays and sheds nearing completion. The form of the filled in bay is clearly visible with the power station and Pirelli Cable Works forming the far boundary. The Southern Railway advertised this as an industrial estate, but for some time the only occupant was Rank's Solent Flour Mill. In April of this year, the press reported that for the first time all the berths had been occupied simultaneously. The laid-up *Mauretania* is the large white-hulled vessel.(*ABP/1825*)

By 1938, when the new General Motors plant opened, the carriage sidings have been installed and Montague L. Mayer Ltd is the only other tenant. Their one-hectare timber depot opened in October 1937. The main road through the estate, named Herbert Walker Avenue after the Southern Railway General Manager, had been opened by the chairman, Mr Holland-Martin, in May 1936. (*Phillips/M19886*)

The Western Docks in the 1960s. The near building is the Cold Store opened at 108 Berth in May 1958. There is a vessel of the New Zealand Shipping Company alongside. (*Phillips/M16490*)

The Ocean Terminal nearing completion in 1950. The building, designed by the British Transport Commission architect C.B. Dromgoole, was a great innovation at the time, and set new standards in the provision of facilities for passengers. (*Phillips/M21059*)

Passengers from a ship the size of *Queen Mary* would require up to five special trains to transport them, with one being a Pullman train as shown here. While second class was abolished on the LSWR after World War One, leaving only first and third, special second-class rolling stock was provided for boat trains to match the provision of the shipping companies. (*Phillips/M19071*)

The platform for the reception of boat trains was within the Ocean Terminal so that passengers could go to the departure lounge above and then to their ship with the minimum of effort. Boat trains ran directly from London Waterloo. (*Phillips/M19070*)

William Crundall & Co's Itchen Ferry timber yard about 1928. The firm continued on this site until at least 1948. (*SCC/M4349*)

The Supermarine aviation works in the late 1920s, on the Woolston side of the River Itchen. This was where Reginald Mitchell developed his award-winning aircraft, including seaplanes that went on to win the Schneider Trophy. (*SCC*)

A feature of the docks often seen and used by passengers was the row of shops on Central Road, just inside dock gate 4 in the Eastern Docks. Some of these businesses continued to operate until the late 1980s, despite having been damaged in World War Two. This picture, taken in 1950, shows the shop of C.R. Hoffmann whose postcards of famous liners fed a public hungry for such material. (*ABP/2450/1*)

Mail and Passenger Connections

AS early as 1825 there was a complaint in the *Southampton Herald* that the smoke from steamers was obscuring the view of Southampton Water.

In January 1841, the first P & O vessels, *Great Liverpool* and *Oriental* moored in Southampton Water. The following year, the *Hindustan* opened a new service from Southampton to Calcutta.

In December 1841 the Royal Mail Steam Packet Company's paddle steamer *Forth* made her first trip from Southampton to the West Indies, followed closely by the *Tweed*, *Solway* and *Clyde*. The Royal Mail Steam Packet Company had been incorporated in 1839 and started its Government mail contract from Falmouth in 1842. However the port of departure for mail was switched to Southampton and when *Teviot* sailed with the first 56 bags of mail for the West Indies, the event was marked by a 13-gun salute from the Platform.

Heading across the Atlantic, *British Queen*, operated by the Belgian Government, had commenced a service to New York from Antwerp, calling at Southampton on outward voyages. Trans-atlantic services were improved in 1847 when the Ocean Steam Navigation Company of New York inaugurated their Bremen, Southampton, New York service with the paddle steamers *Washington* and *Hermann*, joined in 1851 by *Franklin* and *Humbolt*.

On the North Atlantic, the Ocean Steam Navigation Co was taken over by the European and American Steamship Line. The *Vanderbilt* continued to operate from Southampton to New York until she was given to the Union side for use during the American Civil War. There were some sailings to the USA by the Atlantic Mail Company using the ex-Collins' liner *Adriatic*. Two long-standing links were formed, with North German Lloyd from Bremen making Southampton a port of call in 1858 and Hamburg America Line the year after.

The General Screw Steam Shipping Company added to the diversity of companies by placing their *Indiana* on the Mauritius, Ceylon, Madras, Calcutta route in April 1853. In September 1857 the locally formed Union Line commenced a new service handling the mail to South Africa with the *Dane*.

These early years were eventful for other reasons. The Royal Mail Company lost several ships through inexperience and inadequate charts. The *Forth* was stranded in 1849, and the *Amazon* was lost through fire on her first outward voyage to the West Indies. She had been the largest timber-built steamship built in England.

The *Washington*, arriving in New York in November 1853, was placed in quarantine because of an outbreak of cholera on board which killed 100 people. During the 1850s several Royal Mail ships brought cases of yellow fever from the West Indies. *La Plata* had 30 cases, nine of whom died, *Magdalena* lost 12 and the *Trent*, nine.

Larger and more efficient ships were developed during the 19th century, since it had been realised that the larger the hull, the smaller the proportion of space required by the engines so that more capacity was available for cargo or fuel. The wooden paddle steamers of Royal Mail had been large but of a conservative design because of the terms of the mail contract.

P & O were not so constrained and *Pera*, which sailed for her trials from Southampton in 1856, was an iron screw steamer. She had several locally designed innovations, with the patent boilers of Lamb and Summers and a system of movable dining tables designed by a local man named Taylor. An earlier Taylor family in Southampton had devised ingenious tools for the production of standardised rigging blocks, but it is not known if there is any connection with this later Mr Taylor.

Services to India by P & O, gave the language a new word, 'posh', which arose from the habit of better-off travellers requesting cabins on the port side going out and the starboard on homeward voyages (port out, starboard home). Thus these posh people escaped the full effects of the sun in the days before air conditioning.

From 1875, P & O gradually withdrew their services from Southampton, being absent from 1880 to 1925. Other companies stepped in. American Line transferred its operations from Liverpool in 1893 and brought the world's largest passenger ships of the day, the *Paris* and the *New York*, to Southampton. This company initiated a second service from Southampton in 1903, claiming their costs were much reduced when compared with Liverpool and that the London and South Western Railway cargo handling was very efficient.

American Line were innovators, using radio to produce a newspaper the *Marconi Bulletin*, for passengers, providing this first on the *Philadelphia* in May 1903 although Royal Mail followed closely with the *Para Supplement*. News was transmitted to ship laboriously by Morse code, but as late as 1931 the radio broadcast, made at a distance of 700 miles by the Canadian Pacific *Empress of Britain* on her maiden voyage from Southampton, was hailed as a remarkable achievement.

The bulk of the Sea Post Service for the North Atlantic was transferred from Liverpool to Southampton in 1907 coinciding with the move of White Star Line. This was a means of speeding up delivery where postal workers from Britain and the United States sorted mail en route. The scheme was extended to Union Castle ships going to South Africa in 1913, but the whole system was terminated in August 1914 and never restarted. In the late 1920s, there were experiments with catapults on German ships, and from 1929 the *Bremen* launched an aircraft while still out at sea so that the mail could precede the arrival of the ship by several hours.

Competition on the North Atlantic route had always been intense and from the outset, the fastest ships were awarded the coveted Blue Riband as an accolade. In time this rivalry took on nationalistic overtones, but as Southampton was not the only transatlantic port, it only occasionally had contact with record-breaking ships such as the *Kaiser Wilhelm der Grosse* in 1897, until the transfer of Cunard from Liverpool in 1919. The *Mauretania* held the Blue Riband when she arrived and continued to do so until overtaken by the *Bremen* in 1929.

In order to have something tangible to compete for, a British Member of Parliament, Harold Hales, presented a trophy bearing his name. This was held very briefly by the Italian liner *Rex*, and subsequently by only three other liners, commencing with *Normandie*, all of which regularly called at Southampton.

At the time that French Line was constructing *Normandie*, Cunard was also building a giant liner for the North Atlantic. There were various setbacks and Government assistance was required, but when *Queen Mary* arrived in Southampton in March 1936 and was put into dry dock, the public interest was tremendous. A special public enclosure was made, special trains were run and 25,000 people came in one day alone to see this great ship. The enthusiasm continued, for even on her return from her maiden voyage to New York in June, 5,000 people a day were going to see her.

The dry dock used by *Queen Mary* was the specially constructed King George V Graving Dock at the western end of the New Docks. It was a facility that the Southern Railway was reluctant to build as the company felt that it would be little used.

The *Queen Mary* and her sister *Queen Elizabeth*, when she finally came to Southampton, were berthed in the Ocean Dock where a new passenger facility had been planned by the Southern Railway since World War Two. This new Ocean Terminal was opened in 1950 by the then Prime Minister, Clement Attlee.

This was followed closely by a second terminal at 102 Berth that was opened in January 1956 by His Excellency Mr G.P. Jooste, High Commissioner for the Union of South Africa.

Although the Ocean Terminal building was only demolished in 1983, these buildings had relatively short lives because the ocean liner itself had been eclipsed by the air liner. *Queen Mary* bid farewell to the port on 31 October 1967, followed by *Queen Elizabeth* on 29 November 1968. *United States* left Southampton for the last time in November 1969 and six years later the *Northern Star* of Shaw, Savill & Albion, made her final departure. The same year, 1975, the partial withdrawal from shipping of Holland America Line saw the disappearance of their liners from Southampton, and the last South African mail ship SA *VAAL* (the former *Transvaal Castle*) departed in September 1977.

P & O iron paddle steamer *Massilia* photographed in the 1860s. Although not taken in Southampton, this is one of the earliest photographs of a ship that used the port. She was in fact designed for the Southampton-Alexandria service. (SCC/M4072)

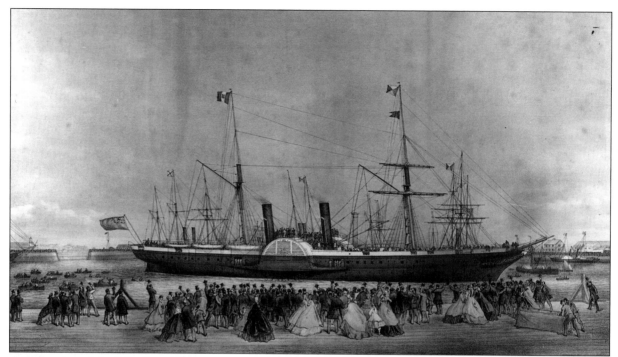

An engraving of the P & O paddle steamer *Ripon* bringing Giuseppe Garibaldi, the Italian patriot, to Britain in April 1864. The ship had been requisitioned as a troop transport during the Crimean War, when she conveyed the Grenadier Guards to the Black Sea, while her sister ship, the *Orinoco*, took the Coldstream Guards. *Ripon* was built on the Thames by Money Wigram and Sons and was lengthened twice in her career, which lasted from 1846 to 1870. (*SCC/M1493*)

Extra bustle in the Outer Dock caused by a dock strike in London in August 1889. The ships are: in the centre the *Arcadia* and in the far distance, the *Magdalena* and the *Drummond Castle*. The row in front of the dry docks comprises, from left to right, *Dee*, LSWR paddle steamer *Brittany*; *Elbe* and *Medway*. (*SCC/M3932*)

Una in the Outer Dock before despatch under her own power to Rio de Janeiro where she was a tender to Royal Mail ships. She was a wooden craft of only 47 tons, built in 1907 by Peckett. *(SCC/M2076)*

American Lines *Paris* entering the Prince of Wales Dry Dock in 1895. At the time this was the biggest dry dock in the world, capable of receiving the world's largest ships. The structure in the foreground is the caisson used to close the dock. *(SCC)*

The White Star, later Ocean, Dock nearing completion in 1910. The presence of the Union Castle liner *Carisbrook Castle* shows that it was already in use. The International Cold Store, which was relatively new at the time, is visible in the distance. (*ABP/TH6/277/5*)

A famous view by Stuart of the ill-fated White Star liner *Titanic*. The loss of the *Titanic*, together with the lives of so many local seafarers, had a profound impact on the town and changed shipping regulations and practice. (*Stuart/M1438*)

A postcard by Hoffmann of *Majestic* in the Floating Dry Dock. (*Hoffmann/22.1982.1*)

An impressive view of the Ocean Dock taken by Kennaway in July 1930 showing some of the largest ships in the world at the time. From left to right they are the Cunard *Mauretania* and *Berengaria*, White Star *Majestic* and United States *Leviathan*. There is a fifth, the Canadian *Pacific Empress of Japan* just visible on the right. Three of these ships are former German craft, taken as reparations after World War One. (*Kennaway/1A90*)

White Star *Homeric* turning with tug assistance. *Homeric* was launched in 1913 as the *Columbus* and, having been acquired by White Star after World War One, made her maiden voyage from Southampton to New York via Cherbourg in February 1922. (*PhillipsM21020*)

Seen here entering dry dock, Canadian Pacific *Empress of Britain* was the vessel that brought King George VI and Queen Elizabeth back to Southampton from their Canadian Royal Tour just before the outbreak of World War Two. The ship was sunk in October 1940. (*Phillips/M20927*)

The Cunard liner *Lancastria* photographed in Southampton in July 1932, having operated the London, Le Havre, Southampton, New York service since 1926. At least 3,000 lives were lost when the *Lancastria* was bombed and sunk off the Brittany port of St Nazaire on 17 June 1940, while evacuating troops. It was Britain's worst single maritime loss of life during World War Two. (*Kennaway/2C15*)

P & O *Strathaird* being painted while in dock in 1932, the year she came into service. During World War Two she served as a troopship, and later returned to civilian operations on the Australian route. (*Kennaway/2D13*)

The *Mauretania* in her white-hull days in 1933. An interesting feature is the collection of coastal tankers and hopper barges around her. (*Kennaway/2.00E+01*)

Ubena of the German East Africa Line forged her links with Southampton in August 1928 on her maiden voyage from Hamburg to Cape Town. Her owners were expanding their service at the time, and she was the second new vessel belonging to the company to call that year. (*Phillips/M20913*)

Europa was one of the express liners of Norddeutscher Lloyd and briefly held the Blue Riband for the fastest transatlantic crossing, until it was taken by her sister the *Bremen*. She went into service, calling in Southampton, in 1928. This picture was taken in 1935. *Europa* survived World War Two and became French Line's *Liberte*. (*ABP/237A*)

The huge ocean greyhound of French Line *Normandie* was longer than *Queen Mary* by a very small margin, and also slightly heavier, and so qualified as the largest ship in the world at the time. She was originally scheduled to stop at Southampton only on return crossings of the Atlantic, but Southampton was soon substituted for Plymouth on outward journeys. Communication with the ship was by tender sent from Southampton, which saved time and reduced harbour dues. (*Phillips/M20897*)

Berengaria was built as the *Imperator*. In February 1938 a serious fire broke out on board and took six fire engines and the fire-fighting tug *Sir Bevois* to bring under control. The next month there was a similar incident in New York, after which *Berengaria* was returned to Southampton and withdrawn from service. This picture is believed to represent her final departure from Southampton. (*Phillips/M20949*)

Norddeutscher Lloyd *Gneisenau*, sister of the *Scharnhorst*, photographed in Southampton in June 1938. She came into service in January 1936 on the Bremerhaven, Southampton, Hong Kong, Japan service. She was sunk by a mine in May 1943. (*Kennaway/4N39*)

Patriotism would have required the use of a German ship to bring these motorcyclists to Southampton. They landed at the Western Docks in 1938 on their way to an event in Wales. (*Phillips/M21414*)

Caronia arriving in Southampton when new in 1949. Known as the 'Green Goddess' from the colour of her hull, she was designed for a dual-purpose Atlantic crossing or cruising role, and was said to be more luxurious than the *Queens*. (*Phillips/M21044*)

Queen Elizabeth entering King George V dry dock in 1946, still in grey but with funnels in Cunard colours. The dry dock was at the extreme western end of the Docks at that time. The isolation hospital is the only major feature beyond. Prior to the construction of the hospital, an isolation unit was provided from 1893 to 1923 by the ship *City of Adelaide* which was moored off Millbrook Point. *(Phillips/M20900)*

Back to peacetime livery and minus the de-gausing apparatus, *Queen Elizabeth* is nudged into 101 Berth in a city that still shows signs of wartime suffering. *(Phillips/M20947)*

Queen Elizabeth being assisted to her berth by tugs, the first bring the tug tender *Calshot* (now preserved). Tendering ships was a big operation. In 1937 for example, 441 ships were met and 27,725 passengers handled. In 1938 the number of ships met was 418, and the number of passengers carried was 28,008. (*ABP/2648*)

Marine Tiger, a standard US troopship, was operated for a short time after World War Two by the United States Line. She carried her passengers in dormitories with men and women segregated. (*ABP/378*)

Not the *Canberra* most people remember, but an earlier ship of that name built in 1913 for the Australian Howard Smith Line. She was bought in 1947 by the Goulandris shipping company and ran from Bremerhaven to Quebec and Montreal until 1954 when she was sold to the Dominican Government and renamed *Espana*. (*Phillips/M21062*)

The Polish liner *Batory* made scheduled crossings of the Atlantic in the late 1940s and 1950s. She made headlines in May 1949 when she sailed from the United States with the East German leader Gerhart Eisler. Although he had been under arrest in America, he was detained only briefly in Southampton before release. The ship was broken up in Hong Kong in 1971. (*Phillips/M20964*)

The United States Line *America*. When Chandris Line took over the Australian migrant contract from Sitmar in 1970, the redundant *America* was used, renamed *Australis*, and in that capacity is reputed to have carried a total of 250,000 migrants from Southampton. She later became a successful cruise ship. (*Phillips/M20957*)

Queen Elizabeth at Ocean Terminal. Both Red Funnel tugs, *Dunnose* and *Calshot*, were built locally by J.I. Thornycroft. *Calshot* was sold to Holland America Line in 1964 while *Queen Elizabeth* lasted only another four years. (*Phillips/M16510*)

Crowds flocked to Mayflower Park in 1969 in order to see *United States* sail from Southampton for the last time. (*Phillips/M16579*)

Cruising

ARTHUR Anderson, one of the founders of P & O was an imaginative man and introduced the concept of modern cruising as 'Tours' from Southampton to Cairo and the Holy Land. He even persuaded the author William Makepeace Thackeray to go on one and write favourably about it, although people did not go to enjoy the facilities of the ship. One traveller wrote that the experience had '…little to recommend it beyond novelty and the P & O claret.'

Between World Wars One and Two, cruising – that is sailing on a big ship for the pleasure of travel rather than to reach a specific destination – became an established activity. Companies that had only seasonal use for their passenger-carrying ships completed their schedules by cruising at other times of the year. Thus B & I Troop ships were employed on cruising between early spring and September when there were no peacetime troop movements, and Canadian Pacific ships that were excluded by ice from the St Lawrence during the winter would be diverted to cruising.

The Aberdeen and Commonwealth Line used their Bay Class ships for cruising at times when they were not all required on the Australian run. Other companies had ships devoted specifically to the trade such as Blue Star Line's *Arandora Star* and the Royal Mail *Atlantis*, the former *Andes*.

Coast Lines claimed that one could cruise round the British Isles in their ships, but this is stretching the definition of cruising. In this case travelling by sea offered a more leisurely way of getting about than could be achieved by taking the train from Liverpool to Southampton. Even today it is still possible to travel on what are primarily cargo ships to destinations served by scheduled airlines.

Cruising then, until the decline of the passenger ship for everyday travel, was a minority activity. With increased leisure, it has become the dominant use of passenger ships and a growth industry.

In the late 1970s voyages by cruise ship were combined with coach travel and journeys by air, so itineraries became more adventurous.

The Orient Line *Oriana* (I) was designed for use in a dual role as passenger ship or as cruise ship and was the first to have a television installation that could receive programmes in different parts of the world. She was also the first to have sideways movement propulsion to enable her to manoeuvre without assistance in far flung places; and the first to have built in baggage loading and discharge equipment. Her P & O successor *Oriana* (II) was the first ship specifically designed for the British cruise market and made her maiden voyage from Southampton on 9 April 1995.

In October 2001, P & O Cruises moved offices to Southampton and in 2003 the new Mayflower Cruise Terminal is due to open, confirming Southampton's position as Northern Europe's principal cruise port. In Britain in 1995, 250,000 people went on a cruise, though this figure will soon reach 700,000.

Millennium, a gas turbine-engined cruise ship completed in 2000 by Chantiers de l'Atlantique at St Nazaire for Celebrity Cruises Inc. This 90,228-tonne ship called at Southampton in June 2000. (*Picsales.com/6904-14A*)

The cruise ship *Arandora Star* was the only vessel of the Blue Star Line to make regular visits to Southampton. She is seen here at the top end of Ocean Dock in May 1931. *Arandora Star* was torpedoed and sunk in July 1940 carrying prisoners of war and internees to Canada. Some 761 people were killed. (*Bealing/M9638*)

Oriana, the first cruise liner designed specifically for the British cruise market, made her maiden voyage in April 1995. P & O now operates four cruise liners from Southampton. (*Red Funnel*)

Migration

ONE can take ships to foreign parts for business or for pleasure, but large-scale migrations are often occasioned by more basic needs and Southampton has played host to many groups that have of necessity passed through the port.

One of the earliest and most notable were those who sailed on the *Mayflower* in 1620 to establish a new life for themselves in America.

There may have been emigration from Southampton to Georgia in the 1730s, but few accurate records exist until the 19th century, when Government-assisted passages to Australia prompted a flurry of activity. Eligibility for assisted emigration to Australia depended on perceived need and in 1852, the most eligible were married agricultural labourers, shepherds or herdsmen, and women of the working class up to 45 years old. Married mechanics and artisans could also get help with the cost of a passage, with single men and families with more than four children being least likely to be accepted.

Also in 1852 a private emigration scheme for families was established by Mrs Caroline Chisholm, using Southampton as the port of departure. She was assisted in this venture by one of the directors of the London and South Western Railway. Her first ship, the *Ballengeich* left Southampton in August 1852. The following year, there were 35 Government and six private sailings including the *Mary Green* in March, for Adelaide; the *Statesman* in July for Melbourne; and the *Joshua* for Sydney.

From the late 19th century, ships crossing the Atlantic often carried steerage passengers from Europe seeking a better life. The *Titanic* was no exception. It is impossible to gauge the level of migration from the monthly *Southampton Docks and Shipping Guide* which listed predicted arrivals and departures from the port, for these were ordinary sailings, not specifically chartered to carry emigrants. The British government still provided assisted passages: an advertisement in the *Daily Mirror* in June 1914 proclaimed: 'Australia for £3 – Government Guarantees Work.'

In 1922, Canadian Pacific, White Star and Cunard joined forces to acquire a disused airfield near Eastleigh, as there was no longer enough space in Southampton to accommodate the increasing number of people emigrating to Canada and the USA. The camp was converted to a hostel for emigrants and named Atlantic Park.

Later, another transit camp had to be set up for refugees from the Spanish Civil War, and in the late 1930s displaced people from Germany were passing through. The *Manhattan* took refugees and £11,000,000 in gold to the USA in March 1939, followed the next month by the *Washington*. The *Jervis Bay* took a group to Australia, and in June the Hamburg America Line ship *Rhakotis* landed 200 more.

The *Mauretania* was demobilised from Government service in January 1919 after repatriating 5,000 Canadian troops from Southampton at the end of World War One.

Repatriating displaced persons and troops at the end of World War Two took much longer, and the considerable loss of ships meant that established passenger routes did not return to normal until the late 1940s. The last duty of *Queen Mary* before finishing her war service was to take the families of service personnel from Southampton to embark on new lives in America.

Aquitania, the last four-funneled liner, spent 1949, her final year, carrying migrants to Canada.

The *Empire Windrush* is well known for having, in 1948, brought 500 people from Jamaica seeking a better life in the UK. On that occasion she docked at Tilbury, but was refitted in Southampton in 1950 and was returning to Southampton from Yokohama with over 1,200 troops, women and children in 1954 when she caught fire and sank, fortunately with very few casualties. Most post-war immigrants arriving in Southampton seem to have used regular sailings.

A Victorian reconstruction of the scene in Southampton on the departure of the *Mayflower*. The pilgrims set out in 1620 to start a new life in America, where they felt they would be free from religious persecution. (*Hallett-Gerrard*)

A contemporary engraving from the *Illustrated London News* showing the *Ballengeich*, the first Australian emigrant ship sponsored by Mrs Chisholm, about to depart Southampton in 1853. (*ILN/M3699*)

When Belgium became involved in World War One, many of its citizens escaped to Britain. The *Southampton Pictorial* photographed some of these refugees in Southampton in 1916. (*Southampton Pictorial*)

Belgian refugees were arriving in Southampton at the same time as German prisoners of war. Here an escorted column of German POW's march from the docks, past the recently-constructed Pirelli cable factory. (*Southampton Pictorial*)

A motley collection of small French craft that had escaped after the fall of France to the Germans in June 1940, moored at 108 Berth. (*Hallett-Gerrard/607/40*)

Refugees arriving in Southampton just before World War Two. These may have been some of the people who came on the Hamburg America Line *Rhakotis*. (*Phillips/M20932 and M20930*)

German prisoners arriving in Southampton towards the end of World War Two. (*Hallett-Gerrard/939/2*)

P & O *Corfu* operated mainly on the London, Bombay, China route from 1931, interrupted by wartime service as an armed merchant cruiser and troop transport, until she was sold in 1961. This picture shows her in Southampton repatriating prisoners of war from Japan on 7 October 1945. (*ABP/5087*)

Both the *Queen Mary* and *Queen Elizabeth* carried the wives and children of American servicemen back to the United States as one of their final military duties. Relationships were maintained by the War Brides Parents' Association. (*Phillips/M16615*)

Empire Windrush, photographed in Southampton in May 1951 in her troopship livery. She started in 1931 as the *Monte Rosa* of the Hamburg South America Line and was converted to a British troopship in 1946. (*Kennaway/5Q39*)

Relatives wave to migrants going to Australia on the Sitmar Line *Fairsea*. She was built in the United States in 1942 as an escort aircraft carrier and converted after the war and chartered to the International Refugee Organisation. In 1955 she was contracted to the Australian Government to carry migrants. (*Phillips/M22315*)

Calshot at 107 Berth in October 1953, returning prisoners of war from Korea. *Calshot* met the troopships *Empire*, *Orwell* and *Asturias* in Cowes Roads and brought the repatriated prisoners to the New Docks to be reunited with their families. (*ABP/3196/4*)

Ferries, Pleasure and Railway Steamers

THE first ships in Southampton to be powered by steam were the local ferries, in an attempt to improve reliability. The Southampton and Cowes Post Office Packet *Prince of Coburg* came into use in July 1820.

A consortium of Jersey merchants purchased the *Royal Charlotte* for ease of communication with Southampton, and put her into service in November 1821, though unfortunately she was lost in a gale two years later. By this time the first locally-built steamer, *Medina*, had been built in Cowes and started a service to Guernsey. *Prince of Coburg* had made a voyage to Le Havre in 1821, but regular services did not begin until King & Co introduced their steamer *Camilla* on the Southampton Le Havre route in June 1824. The French *Triton* was also running weekly between the two ports.

In November 1824 *Camilla* was struck in the paddle box by another vessel and was towed to Southampton for repairs. This would seem to be the first recorded instance of a steam ship being repaired in Southampton. The work must have been effective, for *Camilla* continued in service for some years. The ingenious chain ferry of Charles Rendel was put into service between Cross House and Woolston in November 1836, though the first craft were for pedestrians only. The broad-decked ferry for carrying horses and vehicles was introduced later.

In 1836, the South of England Steam Navigation Co was formed, followed by a competitor, the British and Foreign Steam Navigation Co. Both were operating cross-channel services and amalgamated to form the South Western Navigation Co in 1842, the year the first commercial dock opened. As the name would suggest, there was a railway influence, but railway companies were not permitted to own ships at the time.

When the legislation changed, the London and South Western Railway took over the operation in 1862, although it did not gain control of the docks for a further 30 years. After the railway grouping in 1923, the Southern Railway continued to operate and develop the services, replacing the Southampton-Cherbourg service with a new service to Caen in 1925. These operations concentrated on the Outer Dock. The Continental Booking Office of the Southern Railway has formed an integral part of Canute's Pavilion at Ocean Village, though the area is soon to be redeveloped.

British Railways took over the shipping operations of the Southern Railway after nationalisation in 1948, but these services were withdrawn in the 1960s. The last crossing to the Channel Islands was by the *Isle of Guernsey* in May 1961, and the last continental service to St Malo was made by *St Patrick* in 1964.

Later in the 1960s and 1970s, various continental services were introduced by private operators. Initially based in the redeveloped Outer Dock, now known as Princess Alexandra Dock; some of these services were shortlived, though the first and most significant was launched in 1964 by Thoresen Viking Ferries. In May 1965, the press announced Thoresen 'pioneer 'drive through' principle in Southampton.' Today the Ro-Ro ship is the standard type for cross-channel ferries and ideally suited to needs of holiday traffic, but in the early 1960s the trade was in its infancy and the 'drive-through' vessel was a great innovation.

P & O started a cross-channel service two years later, when Swedish Lloyd also started running ferries to Bilbao. The Bilbao service was taken over for its final two years by United Baltic Corporation, and ended in 1979. P & O started a second service to Spain and Portugal in 1971; Aznor Line offered a service to Spain between 1974 and 1977; and Seagull Ferries ran a lorry service to Le Havre between 1972 and 1975. After a lapse, Stena Sealink introduced a service to Cherbourg which operated between 1991 and 1996.

The Southampton, Isle of Wight and South of England Royal Mail Steam Packet Company began its service in 1860. By the simple expedient of changing the company colours, this became Red Funnel in 1935. This company operates tugs, runs ferries to the Isle of Wight and also operated pleasure steamers. Many of their earlier tugs, which were mostly quite large and with twin screws, had passenger certificates. They were used as tenders to serve ships in Cowes Roads, and 'stood in' at busy times on the other services. Red Funnel first experimented with a high-speed launch, *Island Enterprise*, in February 1935. This made two crossings a day to the Isle of Wight, taking 35 minutes and carrying 11 passengers. This venture was ahead of its time and did not continue, but the company introduced hydrofoils in the 1980s and has since gone on to high-speed catamarans.

The pleasure steamers that survived World War Two were withdrawn in the 1960s. In May 1978 the preserved paddle steamer *Waverley* started to make seasonal visits and so to maintain the tradition.

The *Prince of Coburg* continued to serve as a workshop at Woolston after her engines had been removed. She was painted in this condition by T.G. Hart in about 1840. (*SCC/M222*)

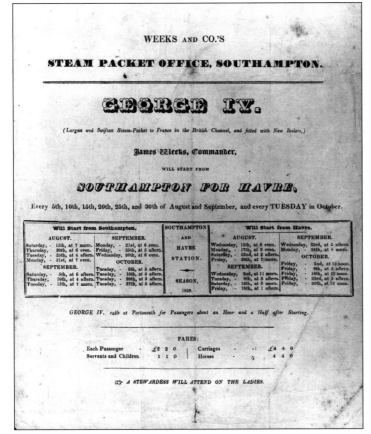

Advertisement for the Southampton-Le Havre steamer service of Weeks & Co of August 1829. (*SCC/2143.198*)

LSWR steamers *Victoria* (left) and *Hilda* beside a set of Day Summers sheerlegs. *Hilda* was completed in January 1883 and operated to the Channel Islands until replaced by the *Stella* after which she operated services to Le Havre and St Malo. She brought General William Booth to Southampton from Cherbourg at the end of his world tour in February 1892 and was wrecked off St Malo in November 1905 with the loss of 125 lives. (*SCC/M3965*)

Prince of Wales and other pleasure steamers photographed at the end of the Royal Pier in the early 1890s. *Prince of Wales* was a product of the shortlived Southampton Naval Iron Works in 1891. The Pier Station, while popular with excursionists, was only accessible to the relatively small rolling stock of the time and was not replaced after World War One. The Pier Station can be seen on the right behind the paddle steamer funnel. (*Borrough-Hill/93.1985*)

The paddle steamer *Solent Queen*, photographed in August 1906 passing the Town Quay. She remained in service until 1948. (*SCC/M2677*)

This postcard of the Floating Dry Dock, sent in 1926, also provides a good illustration of the Hythe ferry *Hampton* built by Day Summers in 1894 and broken up in Holland in 1936. (*Hoffmann/22.1982.1*)

Isle of Sark entering the Outer Dock in August 1934, pictured from the deck of her sister *Isle of Guernsey*. (*Williamson/MM101/38*)

Royal Eagle, the last paddle steamer built for the General Steam Navigation Co., about to leave 103 Berth with a party of day trippers to see the Naval Review at Spithead in July 1935. She is famous for having rescued over 4,000 troops at Dunkirk. (*ABP/3701*)

Southern Railway cargo steamer *Ringwood* photographed in 1947. Built in 1926, she was the last of a series of standard ships introduced soon after the formation of the company and was later adapted to carry cattle. Her last voyage was from Jersey to Southampton in October 1959. (*ABP/M8169*)

A cross-channel ferry that must have brought back memories to some customers. The Townsend European Ferries *Empire Shearwater* photographed in the Ocean Dock in 1958. This ferry started in 1945 as landing ship LST3033. She was broken up in 1962. The other passenger ships in the picture are the Holland America Line *Statendam* and Cunard *Mauretania*(II). (*Phillips/M17227*)

Shearwater 3 of 1972. One of the Red Funnel hydrofoils that provided a 20-minute passenger service to the Isle of Wight. When these craft were introduced in 1969, they provided the only regular hydrofoil service in Britain, but have since been replaced by high-speed catamarans. (*Red Funnel*)

A rather bleak looking picture of the Royal Pier dating from about 1960. This is the new entrance building of 1929, with the lions reclaimed from the previous building. (*Phillips/M19053*)

Red Funnel car ferry *Cowes Castle*, completed by Thornycroft in December 1965, and used for the Southampton-Isle of Wight service. She and her three sisters were modified and lengthened in 1975 to accommodate more cars and became drive-through vessels. The design is derived from a tank landing craft, an example of which was at one time owned by the company. (*Red Funnel*)

Princess Alexandra Dock looking south-west, showing the wide variety of cross-channel ferries that used this dock briefly in the late 1960s. The liner *France* is in the Ocean Dock in the background. (*ABP/2909*)

Flying Boats

A CONTEMPORARY photograph album depicting the inauguration of the first Cross-Channel Air Service to Le Havre in August 1919 describes Southampton as having the world's first Air Port. The term is used differently today to describe any suitable site designed for the take-off and landing of civilian aircraft, not necessarily from water.

This early air service used the four-seater Channel-type plane that had been designed locally by Supermarine as a naval training flying boat. Later a Channel Island mail service was started by British Marine Air Navigation and the service lasted from 1923 to 1929.

1929 was an eventful year because of a visit by the giant German Dornier Do X. The previous year the Fokker Tri-Motor 'Friendship' sea plane of Amelia Earhart had paid a visit following an Atlantic crossing from Newfoundland to Burry Port in South Wales in 20 hours 40 minutes, and taking a further two hours next day to reach Southampton.

The next significant event in regularly organised marine air passenger services was the establishment of a base specifically for the new Imperial Airways 'C' Class flying boats at Hythe in November 1936. *Caledonia* was the first to arrive on a test flight from Alexandria at the end of the year and *Centaurus* took the first passenger flight in January 1937, followed ten days later by *Cassiopea* on the first flight to South Africa. An Indian service was inaugurated in October of that year. Experimental Atlantic crossings were made by *Caledonia* in June 1937 and by a Pan American 'Clipper' III in July, flying via Newfoundland.

Up to this time, passengers embarking from Southampton had been transferred to the flying boat in a tender. A pontoon at 101 Berth in the New Docks was installed to make boarding easier, and the first aircraft to use the new pontoon was *Canopus* in April 1938. This arrangement did not last long, for another move was made to 108 Berth in September. Here the British Trans-Atlantic Air Mail Service commenced in May 1939 with *Caribou* taking 34 hours to New York. Less than three weeks later the equivalent Pan American service started and a terminal building, Imperial House, was opened for passengers.

In early July 1938 an experimental aircraft combination of flying boat *Maia* with seaplane *Mercury* mounted above, arrived at Hythe. The object was to launch the seaplane laden with mail in mid air when part way to its destination, thereby economising on fuel and extending the range. *Mercury* was launched successfully in this way on 20 July and crossed to Montreal in 13½ hours, but the experiment was not continued.

Additional railway lines had been laid between Southampton and Millbrook in 1935 with a connection to the New Docks for boat trains, so when flying boat services became established, special connecting trains were laid on from London Waterloo and later from Victoria.

During World War Two, flying boat services transferred to Poole. On their return in 1948, a new marine air terminal was constructed in the Eastern Docks on the site of the floating dry dock. British Overseas Airways Corporation reintroduced services using new types of aircraft, the Short Sandringham and Solent. Aquila Airways took over after BOAC stopped using flying boats, but operations finally ceased in 1958.

Saunders-Roe had produced the Princess, a prototype long-range flying boat with pressurised accommodation for 220 passengers. Unfortunately the engines available at the time were not sufficiently powerful, and the prototype and two uncompleted craft were eventually broken up following unsuccessful trial flights in 1952–4.

The premises of Noel Pemberton-Billing in Woolston in about 1913. He was a pioneer aviator, was interested in anything fast and had a considerable influence on the young Hubert Scott-Paine who moved from Shoreham to work with him. (*Scott-Paine/M14406.1*)

The pioneering Le Havre service as seen from Town Quay in 1919. (*Scott-Paine*)

Imperial Airways Sea Eagle flying boat photographed in 1928. The Woolston premises of the Ferry Engine Company are in the background. This firm produced marine diesel engines, almost exclusively for the Royal National Lifeboat Institution. (*Scott-Paine/M14399.6*)

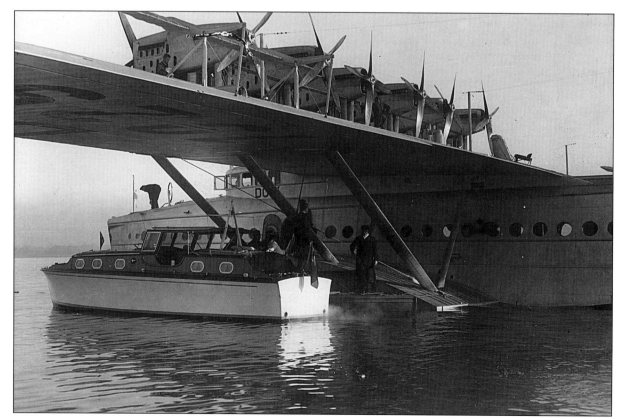

The giant 12-engined Dornier DO-X flying boat on its visit to Southampton in 1928. (*Scott-Paine/M14439.4*)

The experimental Atlantic crossing of *Caledonia* in June 1937 showing the original method of boarding where passengers were transferred from the docks to the aircraft in a tender. (*Scott-Paine/M14436.3*)

Amelia Earhart's visit to Southampton in 1928. She crossed the Atlantic with two male colleagues. (*Scott-Paine/M14399.6*)

Aquatic version of a runway beacon seen at 108 Berth in 1939. (*Phillips/M20936*)

'C' Class flying Boat *Calypso* at 108 Berth in 1939. The guns of the Monitor, HMS *Erebus*, which arrived for a refit in January, can be seen over the cockpit. (*Phillips/M20018*)

Bagged air mail handed over to Imperial Airways staff by the Post Office. (*Phillips*)/M20056

Using a dockside crane, the mail and other cargo is then loaded on to the aircraft. (*Phillips/M20055*)

Captain Caspareuthos of Imperial Airways stands on the quay beside his aircraft. This photograph is significant as it shows the first, and short-lived, flying boat pontoon at 101 Berth, New Docks in 1938. (*Phillips/M19934*)

A Pan American Airways trial Atlantic flight using a Clipper flying boat in 1938, with passengers' luggage being loaded by tender. (*Scott-Paine/M14436.3*)

Loading mail first from a tender on to MAIA and then to the seaplane *Mercury* above, as part of the experimental launch of July 1938. (*Phillips*/M19949)

The Imperial Airways Terminal Building, Imperial House, at 108 Berth as it appeared in 1947. It was used by the US Army during World War Two. (*ABP/1716*)

Inauguration of the Empire Airmail Service to Australia in 1938. (*Phillips/M21466*)

A converted World War Two flying boat being winched into its docking station at 50 Berth in the Old Docks in March 1948. The new flying boat terminal was not officially opened by Lord Nathan until 14 April 1948, when the new Solent Class flying boat *Southampton* was also named by the Mayoress Mrs Dibben. (*ABP/1867*)

Interior of the new terminal building constructed at 50 Berth for British Overseas Airways Corporation passengers. (*ABP/2084*)

The prototype Saunders Roe Princess flying boat seen here at anchor. It is also carrying wheels for bringing on to land. These would not have been carried in normal operation. The wing-tip floats were elevated during flight to form part of the wing. (*Phillips/M19098*)

Fifty Berth and the BOAC Terminal building photographed in 1949 when the Ocean Terminal was under construction. The former Ministry of Munitions Rolling Mill at Weston is in the background. (*ABP*)

Yachts and Yacht Building

PLEASURE craft come in all different sizes to suit individual needs, but generally they fall into two classes: those that are used for pure enjoyment and those used for sport. Often they embody fine craftsmanship and have played an important part in the development of yacht design.

In Southampton, yachting as a pastime was introduced at the end of what is called the Spa Period. The Royal Southern Yacht Club was founded in 1840 with premises opposite the Royal Pier at the corner of Bugle Street.

The rules of the Royal Yacht Squadron at one time excluded anyone with a steam yacht from membership, but this was repealed in 1853 so that powered pleasure craft became respectable.

Southampton had a pool of craftsmen with innovative ideas, and several successful yacht builders operated locally. Because of the range of types of vessel covered by the term 'yacht' there is some overlap with shipbuilders. First in the field must be Day Summers & Co at the Northam Ironworks, followed by Payne's boatyard which was established at Chapel Road in 1841, later becoming Summers and Payne Ltd.

J.C. Fay & Co established the Arrow Yard in Northam, later joining with Mordey, Carney & Co in 1899. In 1912, Fay's Northam Yard became the Southampton works of Camper and Nicholson. J. Stevens commenced in about 1870, becoming Stevens Brothers and then H.R. Stevens & Co on moving to West Quay in 1906.

White Brothers commenced at Itchen Ferry in 1906, being revived as White's (Southampton) Yachtbuilding and Engineering Co Ltd in 1924.

Also early in the 20th century Reid (Southampton) Ltd started building yachts, becoming Alexander Macdonald & Co, Itchen, in 1911. After a spell at Hythe, the successors to this company re-established themselves as R. Kemp in Bitterne Manor from 1930 to c.1956.

More recently the Southampton Launch and Boat Co operated in Bitterne Park from 1929 to c.1960.

J.I. Thornycroft & Co Ltd were yacht builders at Woolston from 1904, though the company had started on the Thames at Chiswick and had a factory for the manufacture of steam road vehicles at Basingstoke.

Some of the largest and most luxurious yachts have graced these waters such as the Royal Yacht *Britannia* and the *Hohenzollern* of Kaiser Wilhelm II.

The 'J' Class yachts of the 1930s were the largest and possibly the finest yachts ever used for sporting purposes, but Southampton remains today 'the home of ocean racing'. Events such as the Volvo Round-the-World Race depart from the City, which, since 1969, has hosted the Southampton International Boat Show.

The availability of lightweight internal combustion engines allowed the development of fast stepped-hull racing craft early in the 20th century. Both Thornycroft and the British Power-Boat Company built types which were ideally suited for military purposes. Hubert Scott-Paine, the founder of the British Power-Boat Co, went on to take the World Water Speed Record in *Miss Britain III* in1933.

The Royal Yacht Squadron Cup Race at Cowes Regatta in August 1853. The winner, *Julia*, belonging to W. Peareth, is on the left followed by Tankerville Chamberlayne's *Arrow*, and the American contestant *Sylvie* of L.A. Depau third. (*ILN*)

Commodore Vanderbilt's steam yacht *North Star* visiting Southampton in July 1853. (*ILN*)

The cutter yacht *Octaroon*, bult by Dan Hatcher in 1862. (*ILN*)

Pente in Fay's Yard. She was built by the company in 1894. (*SCC/M4055*)

Steam yacht *Vanessa* on the slipway at Day Summers. She was built in 1902 for Arthur Bowlby. (*SCC*)

An unfortunate occurrence in Southampton Water. The raising of the steam yacht *Eros*, by the Western Marine Salvage Co, in September 1907. *Eros* was built in 1885 for Baron de Rothschild and while in the ownership of Robert Houston, was struck and sunk off Hythe Pier by the collier *Knightsgarth*. She was repaired locally after refloating. (*Stuart*)

Steam yacht *Sapphire* in Southampton Water *c*.1930. A twin-screw steam schooner, she was built by John Brown of Clydebank in 1912 for Lord Fairhaven, but registered in Southampton. (*Williamson/MM101.82*)

The boatyard of H.R. Stevens & Co after the move to West Quay in 1906. The yard undertook storage and repair as well as building, and their 16ft-racing boats were a particularly successful design. (*SCC*)

Scaramouche photographed in about 1919. She was the favourite sailing boat of Hubert Scott-Paine, creator of many fast boats and aircraft. (*Scott-Paine*)

Panther I was built to the design of Hubert Scott-Paine by Saunders Roe *c.*1929. (*Scott-Paine/M14406.5*)

The Riley-engined speed boat *Whyteleaf III* of Freddy Whyte *c.*1930. (*Scott-Paine/M14406.6*)

Sir Thomas Lipton's steam yacht *Erin* photographed in Southampton Water in July 1930. She was used as accommodation on his last and unsuccessful attempt to win the America's Cup with his 'J' Class yacht *Shamrock V. Erin* was built on the Tyne in 1905, as *Albion*, for the publisher Sir George Newnes and was broken up after the death of Sir Thomas in 1936. (*Kennaway/1B11*)

Left: Candida in July 1930. She was built the year previously by Camper & Nicholson in Gosport for H. Andreae of Portsmouth. (*Kennaway/1A91*)

Right: Sunbeam II photographed in 1932. She was an oil-engined auxiliary screw schooner built by Denny of Dumbarton for Sir W. Runciman (*Kennaway/1C6*)

A 14ft-dinghy race in 1934. (*Kennaway/2F38*)

Bluenose was really a Canadian Grand Banks fishing boat, but her racing potential caused her owners to bring her across the Atlantic. She is seen here in Southampton in August 1935. (*Kennaway/3J5*)

Creole in June 1938, auxiliary twin-screw schooner of Major Maurice Pope, built by Camper & Nicholson in 1927. (*Kennaway/4N38*)

Britannia on her last race in August 1935. A famous composite Bermudian Cutter belonging to King George V, she was scuttled after his death at his request. Originally built in 1893 for Edward VII, she did much to revive interest in yacht racing. (*Kennaway/3H48*)

Astra, a Bermudian cutter built for Hugh Paul by Camper & Nicholson in 1928, and seen here in September 1938. (*Kennaway/4021*)

American yachts *Figaro* from Westport, Connecticut and *Windrose* from New York, cross the Atlantic the easy way. (*Phillips/M16542*)

The former Royal Yacht *Britannia*, seen here with the Red Funnel tug *Dunnose*, dressed for the occasion. She was a frequent visitor during Cowes Week. (*Phillips/M16541*)

Donald Campbell's *Bluebird K7* being loaded on the *United States*. This was in preparation for his attempt at the world water speed record on Lake Mead in November 1955. He achieved a speed of 216.2mph, breaking his own record. (*Phillips/M22326*)

Six-metre Class yachts racing. (*Phillips/M20915*)

In 1953, Sir Alfred Bossom, the MP for Maidstone, presented this Challenge Cup for team racing across the Atlantic. Today the excitement is in round-the-world racing. (*Phillips/M16625*)

Coastal Craft and the Town Quay

THE Town Quay, operated by the Harbour Commissioners, was always the focus for smaller coastal and cross-channel cargo traffic It grew in stages from its position at the foot of the High Street and just outside the Water Gate, and was marked for many years by the gas column. This classical column surmounted by a coal gas flare, which had originally been erected in 1821, was moved to Town Quay in 1829 and has since been relocated to a city park.

The Harbour Commissioners were innovative in their approach to running their own shipping berths and were the first in the UK to introduce electric cranes for cargo handling in 1893.

After the formation of the Harbour Board in 1913, suitable office accommodation was needed. However, World War One intervened, and Admiral Lord Jellicoe finally opened the building, which included panelling from the former White Star liner *Teutonic*, in September 1925. The Admiral was born in Southampton and his father had been a Captain with the Royal Mail Steam Packet Company.

While cargoes of timber and potatoes were the norm, after World War Two there were some vehicle exports including surplus army equipment. The development of the motorway network from the 1960s onwards caused a severe decline in coastal traffic, and Town Quay closed to coastal cargo shipping. Redevelopment for office and leisure use commenced in the late 1980s, although Red Funnel catamarans and Hythe ferries still run regular services from the quay.

The rudimentary Town Quay as it appeared in 1809. The central building next to the Castle Inn was the Custom House at the time, and was replaced in 1847 by the building that subsequently became Union Castle House. Southampton has had a Collector of Customs since 1670. (*SCC*)

The Town Quay as it appeared in about 1880, when photographed by Hibberd-James. It shows a French schooner *Harmonie*. (*SCC/Hibberd Ja*)

A contemporary view of the electric cranes installed at Town Quay in 1893. They were the first such cranes installed on any British quayside. The cranes in the main docks were hydraulically powered at the time. (*SCC/M12292*)

Northam Quay of Dixon and Cardus on the River Itchen *c*.1900. Sailing barges were commonly used for coastal traffic. George Williams, founder of Williams Shipping, started operating from Town Quay using the sailing barge *Spec* in 1894. (*Panton*)

One of the original electric cranes of 1893, No 2 on the east side of Town Quay, performing its last lift prior to dismantling *c*.1950. (*SCC/M12293*)

Nyanza seen at Town Quay in about 1880, showing the line of warehouses which lined the waterfront until World War Two. (*SCC*)

Town Quay from French Street *c*.1880. (*SCC/M9112*)

Town Quay about 1910. A central core of warehouse buildings now extends along its whole length. (*SCC/M4522*)

Taken in July 1937, this view shows the regular use of Town Quay by coastal craft. The Clyde Shipping Company's *Rathlin* is on the left; Coast Lines *Western Coast* has the characteristic black funnel sporting white Vs. (*Kennaway4M43*)

Berend-N, a small coaster from Delftzijl in Holland, sunk at Town Quay. She had been assisted by the Yarmouth, Isle of Wight, lifeboat when she got into difficulties. *(Phillips/M16628)*

Town Quay in about 1952 showing a Coast Lines ship, possibly *Pacific Coast*, and the paddle steamer *Lord Elgin*. The war-damaged end of the quay has been rebuilt by this time. *(SCC/M12271)*

Exporting army surplus equipment, perhaps a little too enthusiastically, from Town Quay in the 1950s. This armoured car has fallen off the ship. (*SCC/M12314*)

A floating crane picking up a new crane for installation at 14 Berth on Town Quay. In the foreground are Allis Chalmers tractors awaiting export to Copenhagen and Stockholm. Regular shipments commenced in April 1950. (*SCC/M12278*)

A comprehensive view of Town Quay in about 1960 showing *Erika Schulte* on the left, discharging chemicals from Canada and *Brigette Frellsen* discharging Swedish timber in the foreground. Behind are *Hada II* from France and *Hasevint* loading for Portugal. (*SCC/M12280*)

The Harbour Board Offices at the entrance to Town Quay in 1947. (*SCC/M12269.1*)

The transit beacons at Town Quay and Royal Pier erected in August 1948 to facilitate the turning of ships such as *Queen Mary* from which this picture was taken. The wartime damage to the end of the quay was not repaired until 1949. (SCC/M12269.2)

Removing the pontoon at the end of Royal Pier. (SCC/M12269.3)

Cargoes

THE early cargoes on Royal Mail ships seem to have been both small in quantity and of little economic importance, but must have been profitable. In the 1840s mercury was taken to Mexico as part of the process for silver extraction and in return currency and cochineal were imported. By the late 1860s precious stones and metals, turtles, India rubber, cigars and ostrich feathers had joined the list of goods passing through the town.

From the creation of the modern Docks, foodstuffs have been an important import. In 1840, before the completion of Outer Dock, the *Eleanor* landed 950 boxes of oranges, which were sent to London by the Southampton Railway and would have been distributed within 24 hours had Sunday not intervened. In 1848 the grape traffic was diverted to Liverpool because of a disagreement over the charges made by P & O. The Guernsey tomato industry, which was established in 1874, added to the diversity.

The usefulness of the railway link to the docks was again demonstrated in May 1909 when the *Tortuguero*, on her maiden voyage, discharged 25,000 bunches of bananas into waiting rail vehicles. The success of this experiment prompted Elders and Fyffes to commence a regular Jamaican service in August 1910. Bananas were imported on the stems on which they grew and special machinery was set up at 24-25 Berths to handle them.

All went well until a major fire destroyed the buildings and 63 waiting banana vans in June 1936, putting 300 people temporarily out of work. However a new shed was built and Fyffes' *Chagres* was the first ship to discharge there in January 1937. A new facility, the Windward Terminal, was created in the Western Docks in 1993 for Geest, but this traffic has now ceased. Fruit is of course seasonal, but different sources ensure a continuous supply, so that, for example, when the North African season ends in May, the Channel Islands season is beginning.

In 1991 a contract was signed with the Federation of Canary Island Fruit Growers for handling vegetables and fruit from the Canaries. As a result a new terminal to handle the traffic was built at 104 Berth. In 1995 the facilities were extended with the provision of new cold storage accommodation. From October to May two or three vessels arrive each week, bringing some 130,000 tonnes of tomatoes, cucumbers, peppers and avocados each year.

The building of the International Cold Store in 1901 further expanded the range of fresh produce imported into Southampton, including meat from Argentina and New Zealand. When built, it was the largest in the world and even in the 1920s there were only two others in Europe that could rival it. Following its destruction during World War Two, a replacement was constructed in the Western Docks in July 1958.

Tobacco was first imported for processing in 1922 for British American Tobacco, the present factory opening in 1926. The finished products are also exported.

The long-standing connection with South Africa brought fruit and gold, and raw materials such as wool, hides and blue asbestos.

At one time coal was brought to Itchen wharves in large quantity and this trade was one of the few to continue during World War Two. As late as 1960, 500,000 tons a year were handled as well as road stone, grain, fertilisers and animal feed. Fertilisers and other bulk cargoes are now handled in the Western Docks, and Britain has become a net exporter of grain with 2,000,000 tons a year being handled in the Southampton silos. The silo at 47 Berth came into full operation in 1982, and that at 36 Berth in 1983.

For many years there has been a two-way traffic in motor vehicles. In the mid-1930s, adapted passenger ships such as the *Westernland* were discharging 70 to 90 General Motors cars per trip. On her second trip from Japan in February 1982, *Kyushu Maru*, a special-purpose Ro-Ro ship, discharged a record 5,540 cars. At the beginning of the 21st century there are some 600,000 vehicle movements a year and this will increase with the new multi-deck car terminal in Eastern Docks due to come into use in 2002.

The creation of a Free Port, where goods can be trans-shipped without passing through customs, added to the facilities of the port in 1984.

Explosion of the brig *Tartar* in the docks in 1843. Action seems to be in progress to sink her in order to extinguish the fire. She was loading guns and ammunition for Mexico at the time of the accident. (*ABP/1754*)

Mechanised goods handling on the LSWR as depicted in the *Railway Magazine* in 1909, with railway company vans loaded directly on to railway wagons for despatch to London. (*Railway Magazine*)

Houlder Brothers *Royston Grange* discharging frozen meat to the International Cold Store in May 1914. (*Stuart/TH2.154*)

The shipping of coinage and bullion has been an important activity. Here, 'specie' is being offloaded for transfer to a waiting ship under the watchful eye of the police. (*ABP/2790*)

Racing pigeons for release were frequently transported to the continent on railway steamers. (*ABP/2801*)

Southern Railway steamer *Haslemere* taking Fossett & Bailey's Combined Circus and Menagerie to Jersey in April 1934. The elephants, which presumably remained on deck, walked up the gangplank without any fuss. The other livestock and equipment were craned aboard. (*ABP/2795*)

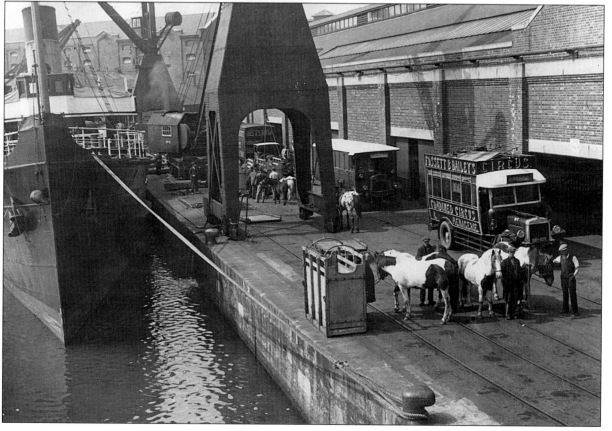

Sunbeam trolleybus chassis going to Johannesburg in 1930s. This traffic continued for many years as the Johannesburg Municipal Tramways Department replaced its entire tram fleet in the late 1950s with 60 very large trolleybuses. (*Phillips/M20974*)

Hororata of the New Zealand Shipping Co discharging at the International Cold Store in 1938. (*Kennaway/4016*)

The Danish East Asiatic Company's *Alsia* photographed in Southampton in June 1938. She displays the Danish flag painted on the sides of the hull to identify her as a neutral ship in the event of hostilities. Like the very first motor ship *Selandia* of 1912, she has no funnel, the exhaust being led up the masts, a practice that has not persisted as it looks decidedly odd. (*Kennaway/4W44*)

The London Midland and Scottish Railway sent an entire streamlined train to Baltimore to tour the United States prior to attending the World's Fair in New York in 1939. Here the partly stripped-down locomotive is being loaded into the hold of the Danish ship *Belpamela* using her own heavy lift derrick. Caught by World War Two, the carriages, which were stowed on deck, never returned. (*ABP/2808*)

Unsound bags of phosphate fertilizer being unloaded from *Norrix* in April 1947. (*ABP/1572/4*)

Road transport in Herbert Walker Avenue in the ownership of British Road Services in the early 1950s. (*Phillips/M19252*)

Heavy-lift ship *Benwyvis* departs Itchen Quays with military cargo. Her derricks, with a lifting capacity of 120 tons, enabled her to transport two Vosper fast patrol boats to Singapore on another voyage. (*Phillips/M17198*)

The wooden barrel has become virtually obsolete for the conveyance of large volumes of liquid as its awkward shape makes assessment of the contents difficult. The instruments shown here were used to check the volume, in this case of Spanish sherry brought by NV *Verdaguer* in 1958. (*ABP/3958/3*)

Grapes being unloaded at 39/40 Berth in October 1958, in a now obsolete form of cask. (*ABP/4030/1*)

Redundant RNLI lifeboat *Helena Harris* from the Isle of Man, being exported to France in 1972. She became a work boat on the River Yonne. Three second-hand lifeboats were also exported to Guatemala on the *Quetzaltenango* in 1958 and heralded the start of a lifeboat service in that country. (*Phillips/M21312*)

Spanish refrigerated ship *Explorador Iradier* docking at 106 Berth. She was sold in 1952, being renamed *Satrustegui*. (*Phillips/M16587*)

This series of three photographs shows the discharge of timber at 40 Berth in about 1957. The ship may be the *Moto*. (*Phillips/M16550 left*).Timber was seasonal traffic from Archangel in Russia and, on this occasion, unloading took ten days. (*Phillips/M16548 centre*). Barges conveyed timber to various yards in the Itchen and to Rea's Wharf at Redbridge. (*Phillips/M16549 right*)

Looking down a hold on the *Windsor Castle* in February 1969. The carefully-stowed packages were often raw materials such as wool or hides. On this occasion they contain asbestos, a major export of South Africa at the time. (*ABP/5698/3*)

The packages of asbestos are unloaded to waiting railway wagons. (*ABP/5698/7*)

Mistletoe, a seasonal traffic from France, was once conveyed in quantity in railway steamers. This picture was taken in early December 1958. (*ABP/4042/1*)

Cable Ship *Sovereign* passing Fawley in October 1991. In May 1975 a new submarine cable depot was opened at 203 Berth. Submarine cables are no longer manufactured in Southampton. (*SCC/M11111*)

Wine tanker *Pointe du Roch* from Brest discharging into road tankers at 106-7 Berth in August 1976, for delivery to the Martin Rossi (now Bacardi Martini) plant in the Western Docks. Today tankers can discharge directly by pipeline and 30 million litres of wine and spirits are handled annually. (*ABP/7338/1*)

Ro-Ro car transporter *Maersk Teal* at 40 Berth in the Eastern Docks in February 2000. Vehicles are now both the main imports and exports from the Eastern Docks. (*Picsales.com/6845-11*)

Dry bulk cargoes being unloaded at 107 Berth in the Western Docks in February 2000. (*Picsales.com/6849-12*)

Containers

AS with many good ideas, the container has been around for a long time. In the latter half of the 19th century there were railway containers of sorts. Before World War One, the arc-roofed box capable of being trans-shipped from road to rail without repacking and therefore much favoured by furniture removers was becoming popular. An advertisement dating from the early 1920s for Shepard Bros shows such a container going by sea to the Isle of Wight.

In 1936 it was quoted in the local press that containers were used for the first time in tendering a liner. The ship was the French Line vessel *Normandie* and mail and stores were brought alongside in tenders, one of which was the *Calshot* which had five containers on board. These were taken on board *Normandie*, emptied and immediately returned. The operation was quick and safe and was judged to be a success.

In 1939 the Southern Railway Company's main exhibit, the dock model, was taken in a container to the World's Fair in New York. There were however, no international agreements on container design and these early examples could not even be stacked one on top of another.

World-wide agreement was achieved at a meeting of the International Standards Organisation in 1961 and the size and shape of container seen today was created. There have been some changes: they are now universally metal in construction; there are new larger sizes; and specialist types have evolved containing for example, refrigeration machinery and liquids.

Southampton was able to take advantage of the needs of container traffic, as they could go directly on some ro-ro ferries from Princess Alexandra dock. By mid-1965, British Transport Docks Board was considering the construction of extensive cargo berths at Redbridge and changing the emphasis from passenger traffic to container freight. Southampton adapted rapidly to the container revolution. Berth 201 was created specially for lift-on containers west of King George V dry dock with the Belgian Line container ship *Teniers* being the first to use it in October 1968. Three further berths came into operation in 1972 forming the Prince Charles container terminal. This has expanded and new specialist equipment, straddle carriers and cranes have been added, as well as new ship berths and a second rail freight terminal to keep pace with demand.

Southampton's container traffic expanded rapidly. In 1968 3,562 containers came into the port and 7,696 left; in 1980 361,707 container units were handled, whereas now over 1,000,000 TEU are handled annually.

Container ships themselves have gone through a transformation. The first generation were adaptations of existing cargo ship designs. By present standards, the second generation, which were the first purpose-built vessels (eg *Liverpool Bay*), were deliberately small in order to pass through the Panama Canal. A third generation of extra large vessels are intended for North Atlantic and Far Eastern services and are also among the fastest vessels afloat, often consolidating cargoes brought in by feeder ships.

At the point of trans-shipment the container is very efficient, so that the loading and turning round of ships in port is very rapid with no awkwardly shaped units to stow or upset the trim of the ship. The role of the shipper does not end as it once did when the goods are deposited on the quayside.

A regular feature in the Southampton Docks yearbook from the early 1920s was this advertisement for Shepard Brothers. (*ABP*)

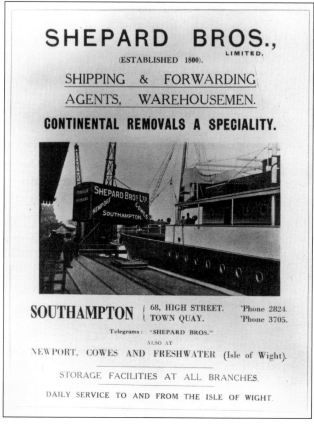

SHEPARD BROS., LIMITED.

(ESTABLISHED 1800).

SHIPPING & FORWARDING AGENTS, WAREHOUSEMEN.

CONTINENTAL REMOVALS A SPECIALITY.

SOUTHAMPTON { 68, HIGH STREET. 'Phone 2824.
{ TOWN QUAY. 'Phone 3705.

Telegrams: 'SHEPARD BROS.'

ALSO AT

NEWPORT, COWES AND FRESHWATER (Isle of Wight).

STORAGE FACILITIES AT ALL BRANCHES.

DAILY SERVICE TO AND FROM THE ISLE OF WIGHT.

The contemporary caption on the back of this 1931 photograph describes '...containers used by the Southern Railway for fast road transport... from Southampton Docks to the principal towns of Hants, Sussex, Dorset and Wilts.' The lorry is a Thornycroft. (*ABP/2447*)

It is the the era of the nationalised British Railways and this same size and design of container is still being used. The illustration shows an insulated container, and dates from about 1960. (*Phillips*/M17267)

Princess Alexandra Dock showing the filled-in Inner Dock used as parking ground, mainly for continental Ro-Ro container traffic in the foreground. This facility came into operation in 1965 using modern type containers. (*SCC*)

The Container Port in March 1983, depicting what was then the busiest day experienced, with five large container ships berthed. In the previous year, 274,851 containers were handled. The berths in the foreground are now used for car traffic. (*ABP/TH6/277/1*)

SA *Sederberg* a few months after she was launched in Bordeaux in 1978 to operate a new container service for the South African Marine Corporation. She was one of a fleet of four vessels and could carry refrigerated containers. (*Vosper Thornycroft /10955*)

Expansion of the Container Port. (*ABP*)

Jervis Bay, with a capacity of 4,038 TEU, entered service in 1992 and has already been replaced by larger vessels. (*Picsales.com/6690-12*)

OOCL *Los Angeles* on the move, showing the reach of the unloading cranes necessary to load and discharge the containers. (*Picsales.com/6897-33A*)

Sail and other Unusual Visitors

A chronicler recorded in 1811 that no large sailing ships, other than Indiamen and men-of-war constructed locally, visited the port, although there were regular sailings by coastal craft to the Isle of Wight, Portsmouth, London, Ireland and the Channel Islands. The small vernacular craft, the Itchen Ferry also evolved as an inshore fishing boat.

It is probable that no large clipper ships visited Southampton, though the matter has been the subject of debate since at least the 1920s. The most frequent sailing ships to call were those built by Oswald Mordaunt, which always came to the docks for fitting out and rigging. The first of these was *Aberfoyle* in 1876.

The boom in sail during the 1880s made little impact on Southampton, but a number of sailing ships bringing bulk cargoes, mostly grain, appear at the beginning of the 20th century. Even then these visitors were noted as unusual, and perhaps the very last to visit was the *Pamir* in 1939.

Some sailing vessels, including the very largest, the *Inverness-shire* of 2,307 tons, were forced to put into Southampton because of storms or collisions. *Inverness-shire* had been carrying a nitrate cargo from Iquique in Chile to Antwerp when she got into difficulties off the Isle of Wight and was towed to Southampton in February 1906. *Sophie* was in collision with the LSWR steamer *Laura* off the Needles in April 1910, and the *Thiers* of Nantes broke her moorings off the Isle of Wight in January 1915 and had to be towed to safety in Southampton.

With the exception of the *Pamir*, which berthed in the New Docks, the grain ships invariably tied up in Inner Dock and Mordaunt's fitting out was done in the Outer Dock.

Coinciding with the sailing grain ships, there was a fashion for using turret ships for bulk cargoes and several of these also visited Inner Dock. They do not appear in many photographs, but Cozens recorded them, the first and smallest being the *Hopedale* of 1895 (1,746 tons) and one of the largest being the *Torrington* belonging to the Tatem

Steam Navigation Co, which called in 1913. The turret ship was produced almost exclusively by Doxford of Sunderland and claimed certain advantages over conventional construction.

The whale factory ship with a stern ramp for taking the catch on board evolved as a type only in 1926. The first were conversions of liners and two Royal Mail Steam Packet Co ships, the *Cardiganshire* and *Carmarthenshire* were so converted, becoming the *Salvestria* and *Sourabaya* respectively.

N.C. Watt's *Southern Empress* operating as a tanker, had discharged fuel here in the summer of 1937. *Unitas*, the factory ship of Jurgens Van Den Bergh Margarine-Verkaufs Union GmbH, then the largest cargo ship in the world, called at the AGWI terminal at Fawley to bunker before going south for her second season in 1938. The fuelling process itself was a record, taking on 21,000 tons of fuel oil in 37 hours.

At the end of World War Two, *Unitas* was taken as a prize and was dry docked at Harland & Wolff in Southampton for repairs, and renamed *Empire Victory*. United Whalers Ltd operated her on behalf of the Ministry of Food until 1950.

In 1946 Southampton was visited by the London registered *Balaena*. The photographs are dated October, which suggests that she was about to go to the Antarctic for the summer.

The British Antarctic Survey commenced in 1943, establishing a weather station at Deception Island in 1944. For many years, the Royal Research Ships and supply ships that relieved the personnel at various bases operated from Southampton and were themselves repaired and replenished here during the Antarctic winter. They were sometimes accompanied by the ice patrol ship HMS *Protector* until her withdrawal in 1982, or foreign survey ships such as the Danish *Kista Dan*, which sailed with the research ship *John Biscoe* in the early 1960s.

The visit of the world's first nuclear-powered merchant ship occurred in 1964. When *Savannah* docked at 101 Berth in July of that year, she attracted 32,000 visitors.

Heinrich of Bremerhaven, photographed in Southampton in 1902. *Heinrich* was built of wood in Maine, USA, in 1875. (*Cozens*)

Tarpenbek of Hamburg at 24 Berth, Empress Dock in 1903. *Tarpenbek* was built in Sunderland in 1892. (*Cozens*)

Tasmania discharging grain in Inner Dock in February-March 1903. The significance of the cattle trucks in the background is a mystery. (*Cozens*)

Holyrood of
Liverpool in Inner
Dock in 1904.
(*Cozens*)

Fahrwohl of Abo in Russia, photographed in Inner Dock in 1905. (*Cozens*)

The Norwegian-registered sailing ship *Sophie* made headlines in the *Daily Mirror* in April 1910, after her collision off the Needles with the LSWR steamer *Laura*. (*Cozens*)

The four-masted barque *Herzogin Cecilie* was built as an officer training ship by North German Lloyd in 1901 when it was thought that all officers needed experience of sail. After World War One she was allocated to the French and sold to Finnish owners, being wrecked off the Devon coast in April 1936. (*Pearce*)

Pamir at 108 Berth in the Western Docks where she discharged 53,000 bags of Australian wheat, an operation that took nearly a month, after which, in July 1939, she sailed for Gothenburg. *Pamir* was lost with all hands on a training voyage in 1957. (*Brocklesby/M3688*)

A fine watercolour of the turret ship *Hopedale* that has just come through the lock into Inner Dock. She was built in 1895 and was sunk in a collision off St Catherine's Point in July 1908. (*Cozens/M13359*)

Turret steamer *Torrington* of Cardiff, arriving in Southampton in April 1913 with Australian grain. (*Cozens/M12517*)

Southern Empress near Fawley when used as a tanker. She continued in this role until sunk on convoy duty in 1942. When compared with *Sildra*, a conventional tanker of the period, the size of the factory ship becomes apparent. (*SCC/M8951*)

Unitas bunkering at Fawley in 1938. (*Echo*/M8948)

By comparison with the present jetty, the pre-war installation at Fawley was relatively small. The stern ramp was introduced in 1926 on the Norwegian *Lancing*. (*Echo*/M8947)

The crew have already started to construct a temporary deck covering using the timber seen here. This is to protect the main deck timbers which would otherwise be severely hacked about during the 'flensing' operation. (*Echo/M8949*)

Stern of *Balaena* showing the ramp. There is a hangar for the spotter aircraft that can be seen with its wings folded. The large crane is for handling the aircraft. (*ABP/63A*)

Balaena in Empress Dock in October 1946. (*ABP/ABP63B*)

The first Antarctic survey ship *John Biscoe*, a wooden vessel built in 1944 as the *Pretext* for the US Navy and renamed when she took up her new role in 1949. She was sold to the Royal New Zealand Navy in 1956 on the arrival of the new *John Biscoe*. (*Phillips/M21063*)

Fawley and Tankers

IN 1921 the Atlantic, Gulf and West Indies Shipping Company started the AGWI refinery at Fawley. By this time oil rather than coal was powering increasing numbers of steam ships, and the motor ship had first appeared ten years previously.

The sea was and remains the most convenient way of supplying a refinery, so Southampton Water was an ideal location.

In June 1921, the first tanker discharged at the AGWI refinery. This was the *Agwilake* of 8,300 registered tons. By 1935, what was then the world's largest tanker, the International Petroleum Co's *Stillman* of 16,434 registered tons had discharged there.

Post-World War Two, a new jetty was constructed and the reconstructed refinery, now owned by Esso, was opened by Clement Atlee in September 1951. The first tanker at the new jetty was, appropriately, the *Esso Fawley*.

Sizes of vessel continued to increase and in December 1956, the press reported the visit of 'the largest tanker to discharge in the United Kingdom'. This was the *Sinclair Petrolore* of 56,000 registered tons.

The jetty, now of 1,500m length has been variously described as the largest privately-owned jetty in Europe, and in the 1960s, was one of the world's largest oil docks. It can accommodate five ocean-going tankers on the outside and can load four coastal tankers on the landward side.

By 1975, the largest tanker berthing at Fawley was the Liberian *Venpet* of 152,372 registered tons, but sizes have continued to increase so that in 1995 the *Hellespont Grand* of 210,658 registered tons, discharged. It is likely, however, that she was not fully laden for her draught would have been too great for the depth of channel. Tanker enthusiasts may claim that the BURMAH *Endeavour* of 213,629 registered tons, which was laid up in the Western Docks between April 1983 and June 1986, was actually larger, but she was empty. Today some 24,000,000 tons of oil and petroleum related products are handled annually.

A rare photograph of a vessel at the pre-war AGWI Terminal at Fawley: the tanker *J.A. Mowinckel*, photographed in 1935. She first visited Southampton in 1933. (*Williamson/MM101/47*)

Olympic Thunder, one of the Onassis Group tankers, built in 1956. (*Phillips/M21296*)

Sinclair Petrolore berthing at Fawley in December 1956, from an advertisement of G. Sharp & Co (Fawley) Ltd. She was then the largest tanker to discharge in the United Kingdom, delivering 52,300 tons of crude oil from Kuwait. (*Sharp*)

The new *Esso Lincoln* berthing at the Esso Refinery in January 1963. The first of a class of four turbine-powered tankers, she was designed for service on the Suez Canal route from the Middle East. (*Esso Petroleum Co Ltd/M8088*)

A comprehensive view of the Esso jetties at the Esso Marine Terminal, Fawley, in 1964, showing the facilities for both coastal and ocean-going tankers. photo. (*Esso Petroleum Co Ltd/CAM643*)

At War

SOME of the forces of King Henry V embarked for France from the West Quay in 1415, during the Hundred Years' War.

The strategic importance of Southampton for military purposes in modern times was recognised soon after the opening of the Inner Dock. The port played a vital role during the Crimean War when ships requisitioned from shipping lines already using the port conveyed troops to the Continent. Ever since, Southampton has come to the fore during times of conflict.

Crimean War

The Coldstream Guards leaving Southampton on the Royal Mail Steam Packet Co's *Orinoco* in March 1854, during the Crimean War. Among the 54 hired transports used during this conflict, the RMSP *Ripon* also played a part, as did the *Mauritius* of the General Screw Steam Shipping Co. She was later destroyed by fire in dry dock in Southampton. (*ILN*)

Zulu War

Pretoria of the Union Line had just arrived back in Southampton from her maiden voyage in February 1879 when news of the defeat of British forces at Isandlwana reached this country. She was immediately converted into a troopship and sailed nine days later with the 91st Highlanders en route for what became known as the Zulu War. (*ILN*)

Boer War

The mineral resources of the Transvaal were exploited by immigrants who were mainly British. Transvaal was surrounded by British possessions and there was a desire at the time to unite the whole of southern Africa. Disagreement over the treatment of the immigrants and the inability to agree a mineral franchise resulted in war.

On the outbreak of war on 12 October 1899, the Government initially requisitioned 101 ships to act as transports and of these 75 sailed from Southampton. Later, other merchant vessels were employed, bringing the total to 267, though this number includes ships of the Union and Castle lines on scheduled sailings but which carried officers, nurses and war materials.

King Edward VII instituted the new Transport Medal for officers employed on transport work though only 154 vessels employed in the conflict qualified for the medal. Captain Smith of *Titanic* fame was a recipient. Officers of ships on scheduled sailings were not eligible.

The king himself wished to present the medals and a ceremony was duly performed in the grounds of Buckingham Palace on 4 November 1903. Captain R.E. Berkeley, RN, the Admiralty Transport Officer for Southampton was kept busy for some time afterwards presenting medals on behalf of the King to men who had been at sea on the day of investiture. His counterpart for the transport ships was Col. Stackpole, Chief Embarkation Officer.

The shipping arrangements at Southampton are often described as being without incident, though this is not entirely true. For example, the Union Castle liner *Mexican* was sunk near Capetown by the transport *Winkfield* and survivors were brought back to Southampton on *Tantallon Castle* arriving 27 April 1900.

Simla was unable to sail with her convoy in February 1900 because of fire. The crew started to deal with it, but had to be assisted by the Docks Fire Brigade. Water froze on the deck and on the tunics of the fire fighters. Deck plates buckled, the deck charred, the troop store room contents were destroyed and a wooden bulkhead burned.

Denton Grange was stranded in March 1900, en route from Southampton to the Cape.

The 6th Army Division, including Field Marshal Lord Roberts, departed from Southampton in December 1899 followed by the 7th Division in January 1900. The 7th comprised 9,688 troops, 552 horses, 18 guns and 37 horse-drawn vehicles and took only seven days to dispatch.

A Remount Depot was established in the docks in January 1900 with a stable for 320 horses. It was run by a veterinary surgeon and 40 civilian grooms.

The *Nile*, the first ship of the Royal Mail Steam Packet Company to take troops to the Cape, was fitted out in Southampton and sailed on 13 January 1900 with 3,000 militia who arrived for embarkation in eight special trains. This was an innovation in coordinated transport.

The P & O steamer *Assaye* on her maiden voyage with the Hampshire regiment, comprising 23 officers and 2,500 men, sailed on 24 January. She was the last ship in the convoy and it was dark by the time she left harbour. This had quite an impact in the press and it was remarked that 'only her many electric lights were visible, making her resemble a floating fairy palace'. Electric light and power was still a novelty at the time, and Southampton did not get electric tramcars until 1900.

Five ambulance coaches were built at Eastleigh by the London and South Western Railway. The extension railway line to Netley Military Hospital having been completed, hospital ships such as the *Maine* were able to discharge their patients directly to ambulance trains in the docks.

In April, *Canada* brought 500 refugees, mostly children from the siege of Kimberley. The Mayor launched a relief fund for refugees from the Transvaal, but the arrival of the sick and wounded caused little interest. The departure of troops was a different matter, and was marked with bands and huge crowds waving. The astute Donald Currie used the departure of Lord Roberts on his ship *Dunottar Castle* on 17 March 1900, as an opportunity to hoist the house flag of the newly created Union Castle Steamship Co for the first time.

All together there were 895 shipping movements into and out of the port conveying 25,384 officers, 502,616 men, 27,922 horses as well as equipment, stores, ammunition and refugees.

It is perhaps surprising that the Boer leaders Botha, De Wet, and De la Rey were greeted with the same enthusiasm as the British generals when they later landed in Southampton.

Part stripped-down Fowler traction engines being loaded as deck cargo on Houlder Brothers' *Denton Grange*. (*Furness, Withy*)

Houlder Brothers *Denton Grange* loaded 7,200 tons of stores for the Army in December 1899. These comprised: 13 traction engines, two steam ploughs, 60 ambulance vans, 170 forage and living vans, 20 ammunition vans, 170 buck wagons, 1,000 tons of hay, and 1,000 tons of oats and bran. (*Furness, Withy*)

The *Denton Grange* was also fitted out with stables for 159 horses. This is the scene below decks before the arrival of the animals. (*Furness, Withy/HB/26/2*)

A Boer War troop train entering the docks. This was the first conflict in which there was co-ordinated use of trains, both to bring troops to waiting ships and to despatch the wounded to hospital. (*SCC/M7067*)

Kildonan Castle leaving Southampton on her maiden voyage in November 1899 as Troop Transport No 44. She was the last steamer built for the Castle Line before the amalgamation with the Union Line. She made three trips from Southampton before becoming a detention centre at Simonstown for prisoners of war. (*SCC/M11816*)

Roslin Castle of the Castle Line in her role as Transport No 26. She sailed a fortnight before *Kildonan Castle* in October 1899, with 77 officers, 1,057 men, six horses, 18 vehicles and one gun. (*SCC/M10486*)

Rippingham Grange loading horses at Southampton Docks in 1900. The ship in the background is a Castle vessel and may be the *Carisbrook Castle*. (Furness, Withy)

Nubia II, of P & O, was Transport No 4. and took 50 officers, 1,614 men, seven vehicles and one gun from Southampton to the Cape in October 1899. She was wrecked north of Colombo in June 1915. (*SCC*)

Manchester Merchant, one of three Manchester Liners vessels that visited Southampton during the Boer War. She was Transport No 92 and is depicted at 30 Berth. In January 1903 she was burnt-out and scuttled in Dingle Bay. (*Cozens*)

Arthur Cozens made copious notes and sketches of the wide diversity of shipping that visited Southampton during the Boer War. This is Transport No 35, *Glengyle* of McGregor, Gow & Co, Glasgow. She made at least one voyage from Southampton in March 1900. (*Cozens*)

Mahratta from the quayside. Most of the ships requisitioned were relatively modern general cargo vessels of about 5,500 tons. Many had electricity and a number were fitted with refrigeration plant. *Mahratta* was built for Brocklebank of Liverpool in 1892 and was Transport No 94. (*Cozens*)

Anchor Line of Glasgow provided three ships, including *Persia*, Transport No 54. Apart from *Britannic*, she was one of the oldest ships involved, having been built in 1883. (*Cozens*)

Horse accommodation on the deck of the *Surrey*. She was a Federal Steam Navigation Co ship, noted along with her sister *Kent,* for taking New Zealand forces to Cape Town. Curiously, her officers were not awarded the Transport Medal although those of the *Kent* were. (*Cozens*)

Britannic I was a pioneering visitor of the White Star Line, appearing as Transport No 62 at the end of her working life. She made three trips from Southampton to South Africa in 1900, and after a period in Australia, repatriated New Zealand troops from South Africa in August 1902, before being broken up. (*Cozens*)

World War One

The smooth handling of exceptional human and other cargoes during the Boer War may be seen as a practice run for the activities of World War One. The jingoism of the previous conflict, while evident elsewhere, did not transfer to the docks. Where previously there had been emotional send-offs and triumphant receptions for military leaders with the Mayor and civic dignitaries often involved, all but necessary workers were now excluded, and an air of secrecy prevailed.

Much of the visual information that Cultural Services owns relating to the docks comes from the work of Arthur Cozens, a clerk, a lover of ships and a talented amateur artist. Commencing in about 1890, he drew and sometimes painted much of what went on, and in fact sketched every transport, troopship, liner and hospital ship operating from Southampton during the Boer War. His watercolours are particularly informative because they give us colour, which no photograph of the time could. Unfortunately, during World War One he could make no records, although he never left his employment in the docks.

Immediately on the outbreak of war the Government took over the operation of the main docks, declaring Southampton a Special Port for embarkation and closing it for Imperial Purposes to ordinary mercantile traffic. In fact Town Quay remained open to coastal traffic for much of the war and was important for bringing in foodstuffs as well as materials for war work.

The Pier also remained open although there was a blackout, which hampered fishing and dredging activities. Vessels employed on Government work did not pay any harbour dues and the Harbour Board immediately set about establishing their loss of revenue and seeking restitution from the Treasury. To assist in their claim, a count of transport ships using Southampton was made and was found to be 1,017 to the end of 1914; 2,666 in 1915; and 3,133 in 1916. No further count seems to have been made.

On the declaration of war, ten Union Castle ships were got ready at Southampton and within two weeks had conveyed a large part of the First Expeditionary Force to France. In fact the first British troops to be landed on 10 August 1914 were from *Dunvegan Castle* and *Norman*. The departure of these 'Old Contemptibles' was commemorated by a plaque near Dock Gate Four.

At the commencement of hostilities, the guard ship HMS *Hermione* was stationed at the entrance of the harbour near Hamble Point, the Harbour Board launch was requisitioned by the Admiralty Transport Department and the steam yachts *Albin* and *Eileen* were requisitioned by the Government.

As time went by, more noticeable changes took place. In February 1915, the Royal Engineers built a 300ft siding adjacent to a new stores building named Roberts Hall, on the Platform. The sidings were lengthened later in the year and the building in 1918. The Ministry of Munitions, having acquired land at Weston from the Dock Company in 1916, stated their intention to build a 770ft jetty there.

Towards the end of 1916, the War Department invoked the Defence of the Realm Act and took over the upper floor of 'B' warehouse on Town Quay and the West Arm of the Royal Pier. On 14 June 1918 the Harbour Board was informed that the War Department was taking over the whole of Town Quay and its warehouses. Fortunately this did not last long, for Berths 13 and 14, and 'J' warehouse were returned at the end of April 1919, with 'A' warehouse following the month after.

What exercised the Harbour Board in April 1917 was the discovery that a military jetty was being constructed adjacent to the Royal Pier. Board members were persuaded that it was both necessary and temporary, and availed themselves of a tour of the jetty and one of the train ferries on 25 July 1918. They then embarked from the Royal Pier to examine the limits of their jurisdiction using the Union Castle launch, *Falcon*. The train ferries ran to Dieppe with urgent replacement guns, tanks, locomotives and machinery, using a direct rail connection to the jetty from Southampton West Station. In eight months, they also carried 17,686 railway wagons loaded with stone and chalk.

Between 6 December 1918 and 8 January 1919 the public were able to examine two captured German submarines exhibited at the Pier and over 16,000 people took the opportunity to do so.

At the Southampton works, Harland & Wolff handled several hundred vessels including refits to 37 patrol craft, 17 monitors, 16 destroyers and four torpedo boats. Twenty ships that had been damaged by mines or torpedoes and a similar number damaged by collision were repaired. The remainder of the work was in converting and adapting existing ships as transports, armed merchant cruisers and 'mystery' ships.

Thornycroft contributed to the war effort by producing 202 patrol boats and seaplane tenders; 114 coastal motor boats; 29 destroyers; 4 seaplane lighters; 4 salvage tugs; 3 submarines; and the decoy or 'mystery' ship HMS *Hyderabad*. Day Summers, which by then had passed its peak in terms of producing big ships, built boom defence vessels, minesweepers, tugs, and a series of special barges for Mesopotamia as well as overhauling 369 ships.

All together the following passed through Southampton: 8 million officers and men; 800,000 horses and mules; 180,000 vehicles; 15,000 guns; 6 million tons of stores; and 7.5 million bags of mail.

Torpedo damage to *Gloucester Castle* visible after she was brought to Harland & Wolff in Southampton for repairs in 1915. (*H & W*)

This is Train Ferry No 3, pictured in 1919. She was one of the rather ponderous ferries that conveyed railway rolling stock to and from Dieppe and, after World War One, brought back materials and equipment. (*SCC/515.1984*)

Margaux entering Trafalgar Dry Dock with bow damage. (*H & W*)

Panoramic view from Ocean Dock to Town Quay taken in 1919. Apart from the row of laid-up warships in the distance and the curved extension to the Harland & Wolff buildings, there is little to indicate the flurry of activity that took place during the war. (*H & W*)

Dazzle paint was devised for ships by the war artist Norman Wilkinson in order to break up their outline and make the ranging of torpedoes difficult. Even in the days before radar it did not always work. This is the *Corton*, following a torpedo attack in 1918. (*H & W/M10107.5*)

Bayronto and *Armenia* together in Trafalgar Dry Dock. There was a steady flow of war-damaged vessels passing through Harland & Wolff in 1918. (*H & W/M10107.5*)

Under repair at the same time as the Train Ferry were the Union Castle liner *Gascon* and the Coast Lines vessel *Devon Coast*. There is nothing in this general view to indicate any impact of the recent flurry of war work. (*H & W*)

Decoy or 'mystery' ship HMS *Hyderabad*. She was the only ship of this type built by Thornycroft during World War One. She looked like an unarmed merchant ship, but had concealed guns and therefore was able to fight back if attacked by submarine. The drawing is a contemporary one by Fred Taylor. (*Thornycroft/M11454*)

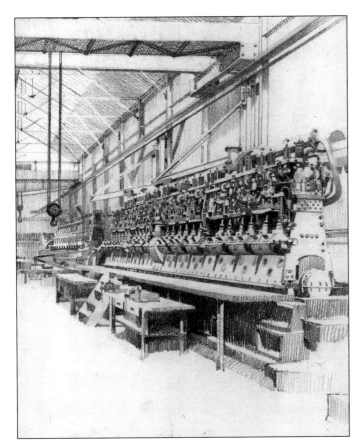

Submarine engines under construction at Thornycroft's Woolston works during World War One. Although Thornycroft built only three complete submarines during the war, these 1,200hp engines were produced for other ship builders. (*Thornycroft/M11451*)

Hospital Ship *Salta*. She used the jetty at Netley Military Hospital which was built to receive the wounded directly from ships, although after 1901 the usual practice was to transfer the wounded to trains at Southampton Docks to avoid vessels grounding at low tide. (*SCC/515.1984*)

Britannic, the sister of *Olympic* and *Titanic*, as an hospital ship. The escort vessels have been crudely obliterated in this censored photograph. (*Moody/2MM113*)

A panoramic view of Thornycroft's Woolston works drawn by Fred Taylor, showing the hotbed of activity towards the end of World War One. (*Thornycroft/M11450*)

Previous picture and above: Olympic photographed in Southampton Docks when in use as a troopship. She is still in her peacetime black, white and buff livery, not yet having received her dazzle paint. (*Borrough-Hill/M6414 and M6415*)

World War Two and after

There had for some time been a sense that war was imminent. Refugees and large quantities of foreign currency had been leaving Europe, often passing through Southampton en route to the United States. There was also an increase in military traffic, gas masks had been issued, barrage balloons were in place and Southampton was blacked out on 10 August 1939. On the last visit of the *Bremen* on 30 July 1939, she was met by the tender *Greetings* off Bembridge on the Isle of Wight and was not let inside the boom defence area; otherwise many shipping activities seemed normal even after war was declared on 3 September.

The first major impact of the war on Southampton was the Dunkirk evacuation at the end of May 1940. The Channel Islands ferry service had continued up to this time and the *Isle of Sark* was the last ship to leave before the German invasion of the islands at the end of June that year.

Between 6 November 1940 and 22 June 1942, there were 12 air raids that impacted on the docks. Several sheds were lost; two tugs and a paddle steamer were sunk and other craft including the hospital ship *Llandovery Castle* were damaged. Rail communications were disrupted, but the quay walls were relatively unaffected. Damage to the town and docks was very severe and, in order to boost morale, King George VI visited in December 1940 and the Prime Minister, Winston Churchill, the month after.

Railway staff working in the docks were moved to temporary accommodation near Andover and work commenced on the building of a part-submerged bomb-proof and gas-proof control bunker in the Eastern Docks.

In 1942, the United States Army Transportation Corps established its operations as US 14th Major Port in the Western Docks and Lease Lend shipments began to arrive in February of that year.

Following the bombing of the Supermarine aircraft factory, the Admiralty took over part of the site in the summer of 1943 and converted it into HMS *Abatos*. This was to be the main base for the Pipe Line Under the Ocean (PLUTO) force for the eventual supply of fuel direct to forces in mainland Europe. Southampton was also the base for the operation for the recovery of the pipelines in 1948–9.

The larger components of Mulberry Harbours were constructed in the docks and there was a build up of all types of landing craft for the planned invasion force. Some smaller craft were made in the Eastleigh railway works and brought by road and rail to the docks in 1943. Others were assembled from prefabricated components brought from the United States. From the departure of this armada in June 1944 to the end of the war in Europe in May 1945, the port handled: 2,840,346 troops; 257,580 vehicles including tanks; 20,516 railway wagons; 770 locomotives; 39 ambulance trains; 22 breakdown trains; and 16 mobile workshops.

On 25 June 1945 the *Isle of Guernsey* re-established the Channel Islands ferry service almost five years to the day since her sister the *Isle of Sark* had departed. American Export Line operated a shuttle service between Le Havre and Southampton with their *Exchequer*, bringing US troops back to be billeted at Tidworth until troopships to repatriate them could be found.

Troops involved in the Korean War of 1951–2 and the Suez crisis October-December 1956 passed through Southampton. The next major conflict was the Falklands War of April-July 1982, when Southampton was the port of embarkation for the Falklands Task Force.

A column of troops of the British Expeditionary Force marching into the docks by Gate 4. (*ABP*)

A Southern Railway photograph of troops leaving Waterloo Station for Southampton. These troops formed part of the British Expeditionary Force which later had to be evacuated from Dunkirk. (*ABP/9943*)

Warehouses on the north side of Inner Dock, destroyed during an air raid in November 1940. Fire hoses still play on the smouldering remains. (*Hallett-Gerrard/2200/40*)

Because of its great size, the bombing of the International Cold Store in 1940 was a major blow to national food supplies. (*Hallett-Gerrard/932/40*)

The bombing of the docks not only caused disruption, but of course also put staff at great risk. The office staff were evacuated in December 1940 to converted railway carriages located at Fullerton Junction near Andover. (*ABP/500[6]*)

King George VI inspects the damage to the Docks in December 1940, accompanied by Mr Biddle, the Southern Railway Docks manager, and civic dignitaries. (*Hallett-Gerrard/726/41*)

The Union Castle liner *Llandovery Castle* as an hospital ship. She was damaged during one of the early air-raids in November 1940, while at 44 Berth. (*ABP/5084*)

Arrival of United States troops at New Docks in 1942. (*ABP*)

The dock telephone exchange having been destroyed, a new control centre, 'N' Vault, was constructed in 1942. Some of the reinforcement of this part-submerged structure can be seen, together with the ventilation shafts in the background. (*ABP/665/8*)

An interior view of 'N' Vault, which, although disused, remained in the car park of what was the Dock Offices until it was finally demolished at the beginning of the 21st century. (*ABP/675/1*)

Railway steamer *Isle of Guernsey* in dazzle paint prior to the invasion of Europe. She was used as a landing ship, and carried her LCA landing craft over the side. (*SCC*)

Tank landing craft assembling at the docks in May 1944, prior to D-Day. (*ABP/M12308*)

US soldiers gathering in Southampton docks prior to D-Day. (*Echo/1285/44*)

British equipment, in this case a bren gun carrier, at Western Docks. (*ABP*)

Prime Minister Winston Churchill visiting the troops shortly before D-Day. (*Hallett-Gerrard/887*)

Tug *Nyati* in Inner Dock after the rubble of the bombed warehouses had been cleared. This at least gave an unobstructed view of the South Western Hotel, which, having been taken over by the Royal Navy in 1940, never returned to its original use. It became the offices of Cunard, but has now been converted into apartments. *Empire Taw* is behind. (*Phillips/M21278*)

Constructing concrete caisson in Southampton Docks. This Mulberry Harbour component, a 'phoenix', is seen nearing completion in 1944. They were made in Dry Dock No 5 and were used as breakwaters. (*Hallett-Gerrard/2657/44*)

Completed dock section of a Mulberry Harbour under tow, surrounded by tank landing craft. This is a 'whale', which, together with 'spuds' and 'rhinos', were assembled near 109 Berth. (*Hallett-Gerrard/893/1*)

Royal Mail Line *Atlantis* in December 1944, in her wartime role as an hospital ship. She is assisted by tug tender *Calshot* in grey and still sporting anti-aircraft guns, back in Southampton after service on the Clyde. (*ABP/53A*)

Queen Elizabeth showing her remarkable troop carrying capacity. (*SCC*)

Empire Taw was built in 1921 as the *London* for the Dundee, Perth and London Shipping Company. In 1942 she was converted to an auxiliary cable layer HMS *Holdfast* and took part in the PLUTO (Pipe Line Under The Ocean) experiments.Seen in Southampton in 1949, she was used by the Ministry of War Transport to recover the PLUTO pipelelines. (*ABP/2233/1*)

The last of six coils of recovered PLUTO pipeline being put down in a bombed shed at 102 Berth in 1949. (*Ingram/2MM99/3*)

After her conversion from a tramp steamer in 1943, *Empire Ridley* and her sister became the largest cable-laying ships in the world, capable of carrying 100 miles of PLUTO pipeline. As HMS *Latimer* she laid the first length, and is seen here on the recovery operation. (*Ingram/2MM996B*)

Unveiling of the plaque given to the Southern Railway by the US 14th Major Port in recognition of its contribution to the war effort. The plaque was presented by the Port Commander, Colonel Sherman Kiser on the right, and received on behalf of the railway company by the Docks Manager, Mr Biddle, on the left. (*PhillipsM19913*)

Pipeline marker buoy being stowed on *Empire Ridley*. (*Ingram/2MM99/12*)

Tug Tender *Calshot* is seen here, having conveyed troops from the Isle of Wight to 107 Berth. These Royal Artillery soldiers then joined the waiting troopship *Dunera* to sail to Suez in 1956. (*Echo*)

The ill-fated RFA ship *Sir Galahad*, loading equipment for the Falklands in May 1982. (*Echo/7326G/3A*)

Troops returning from the Falklands on the P & O liner *Canberra* at the end of the conflict in July 1982. The rust-streaked *Canberra* received a tumultuous welcome. (*ABP*)

The shell of Holy Rood Church, bombed in World War Two, has been preserved as the Merchant Navy Memorial and thus continues to represent seafarers. The Falkland Islands Memorial Plaque. (*Williamson/TH6/277/3*)

Returned components of the Mulberry harbours are increasingly difficult to find, but these concrete 'beetles' were photographed consolidating the foreshore at Marchwood in 1984. (*SCC*)

Until the mid-1980s, roadway sections of former Mulberry Harbour were used at Town Quay for accessing Isle of Wight ferries. (*SCC*)

Trooping and Marchwood

HAVING proved its worth during national emergencies and having the trade routes that it already possessed, as well as proximity to Aldershot, it was perhaps inevitable that Southampton would be recognised as an ideal port for peacetime troop movements. Southampton was eventually designated the Principal Military Port of Great Britain in 1894.

The Government had long standing arrangements with P & O, the British India shipping company and the Bibby shipping line of Liverpool, for the provision of specialist troopships.

In 1866, the Royal Navy also introduced a series of five troopships specially to convey troops to and from India and it was from these that the standard peacetime troopship livery of white hull with a blue band and yellow funnel evolved. At least one, HMS *Malabar*, visited Southampton.

The *Southampton Times* reported that the P & O troopship *Victoria* left Southampton in September 1894 under the new Admiralty regulations for the first time. During the 20th century, the ships of Bibby and BI dominated, with some additional ships being operated for the Ministry of Transport in the period immediately after World War Two.

Troops and their families continued to be conveyed to and from their various posts in a season that operated between September and early spring. When the Bibby Line *Dorsetshire* docked in Southampton on 6 September 1937, there were no less than seven troopships present. These movements continued until the advent of suitable air transport. The peacetime conveyance of troops by sea was discontinued in 1962, with the last voyages being made by Bibby's *Oxfordshire*, sailing to the far east on 18 September and then to Malta, returning on 19 December. *Oxfordshire* eventually became the *Fairstar* of Sitmar Line.

Trooping /Marchwood

This 1930s illustration shows the departure of the King's Own Scottish Borderers. In peacetime, troops' families accompanied them on foreign postings. (*ABP/2966*)

Lifeboat drill on board *Neuralia* in Southampton Docks in 1935. *Neuralia* sank off Italy in May 1945, after striking a mine. (*Williamson/MM101/86*)

Nevasa photographed in July 1935. She survived World War Two and was broken up in 1948. (*Kennaway/3H17*)

Red Funnel tugs *Sir Bevois* and *Calshot* passing *Dilwara* at Itchen Quays, *c*.1936. (*Targett*)

Bibby Line *Dorsetshire* photographed by Kennaway in Southampton in 1938. (*Kennaway/4014*)

Somersetshire departing 20 Berth in the Empress Dock in 1938. (*Pearce*)

Neuralia in BI colours. (*Bell*)

A fall of snow provides an opportunity for amusement when disembarking from a troopship. (*Phillips/M20930*)

British Expeditionary Force troops embarking. (*Phillips/M21475*)

Two Ministry of Transport troopships, *Empire Windrush* and *Empire Ken*. As the *Ubena*, *Empire Ken* was well known in Southampton before World War Two. Her last voyage was from Cyprus to Southampton in September 1957, when she was operated by Royal Mail Lines. (*ABP/220A*)

British India troopship *Nevasa* prior to her withdrawal as a troopship in October 1962. She subsequently became an educational cruise ship for ten years and was broken up in 1975. (*SCCM8167*)

Marchwood

The Military Port at Marchwood was designed and built by the Royal Engineers in 1944 to supply the Allied landings in Normandy. The main gates of the military port were once made from components of Mulberry Harbours brought back from France, however these have been removed in more recent times. Between 1969 and 1979 the stevedore training vessel *Marchwood Freighter* was based here, but changed circumstances rendered it redundant. The Military Port continues today to handle supplies and equipment, often using chartered craft. Its jetties were extensively remodeled by Costain in 1988.

A jetty at Marchwood Military Port in the 1950s. (*Marchwood*)

Two Rea steam tugs at Marchwood in the late 1950s. (*Marchwood*)

Empire Stevedore, the former German Kriegstransporter KT3, was used for stevedore training at Marchwood from 1950 until 1959. She was replaced by *Marchwood Freighter*, a former General Steam Navigation Co vessel that lasted in this role until 1969. (*Marchwood*)

The main gate to Marchwood Military Port as it appeared in 1984. The gateposts were fabricated from Mulberry Harbour floating bridge sections to symbolise the port's origins, but have since been replaced. (*SCC*)

Construction of new jetties at Marchwood by Costain in January 1988. (*CostainMM297.1*)

Services

LORD Sterling said about the transfer of his company's cruise operations to Southampton '...providing the logistical and other support services for a cruise liner... is a huge business.' In addition to repair facilities, every conceivable service is required to maintain and turn round big ships.

Both Royal Mail and P & O had 'factories' in Southampton, where many of their own stores and provisions were kept. Charles Dickens visited the P & O facilities in 1852 and wrote of going '...through forests of brushes of all sorts, sizes and descriptions; lakes of paint; more oil cans than would have concealed the Forty Thieves; museums of pickles and jellies; stacks of spare spars; mountains of sailcloth; piles of carpets, rugs, blankets, counterpanes; showrooms of glass and crockery; floors of elegant chairs, tables and drawers; cabinet work and upholstery enough to suggest the notion that the Peninsular and Oriental Steam Navigation Company's navy are always about to marry...'

Cunard's *Aquitania* was converted to oil burning after World War One and British Mexican Petroleum Co Ltd, established a depot in Southampton to cater for the needs of both Cunard and White Star. Also in the early 1920s the Anglo-Persian Oil Co Ltd established a presence and AGWI. Petroleum Corporation Ltd set up a bunkering and refining facility at Fawley. A review of Southampton facilities by the *Daily Telegraph* concluded that not only did the fuel oil depots contribute to the prosperity of the port, but that 'both coal and oil bunkering are carried out with great dispatch'.

Southampton was perhaps unique in having been able to support the nurseries of the Bealing family who supplied palms and floral arrangements exclusively for liners for many years.

Between 1914 and 1962, when the practice was outlawed, the firm of Andrews operated 'mobile filling stations' to meet anyone importing a car on a liner and who found their vehicle deposited on the quayside without fuel.

Hibberts Brewery was a familiar feature in Southampton for 80 years. This firm had both a bonded warehouse and a bottling plant in the docks and supplied major shipping companies including White Star (the *Titanic* carried Hibberts' beer) and Union Castle. What is perhaps less well known is that in 1957, Hibberts bottling plant claimed to be the first in the UK to put beer in modern cylindrical tins.

The local Trinity House Pilots in 1897. Pilotage was originally started by fishermen and was later regulated by the Merchant Navy Shipping Act, 1894 and the Pilotage Act, 1913. All ships using the port require a pilot. (*Pilots/10.1987.1*)

The local pilots in 1926. Pilotage continued to be a Trinity House function until control was handed over to the Harbour Authority in October 1988. (*Pilots/10.1987.2*)

Pilot Boat 49 coming alongside *Galway Bay* (*Calshot*) on her return to Southampton in 1987. (*SCC*)

Calshot was built as a tug tender by Thornycroft in Woolston, for the Southampton, Isle of Wight and South of England Royal Mail Steam Packet Co, and entered service in 1930. She is shown here in her early form. (*ABP/117*)

The tug *Wellington* of the Alexandra Towing Co at Ocean Terminal *c.*1950. The Alexandra Towing Co, attracted by the move of Cunard, established a base here in 1919. Initially the company stationed five tugs in Southampton including the tender *Flying Kestrel*. Today the company is part of an international organisation based in Australia. (*Phillips/M21060*)

The shelter deck of *Calshot* was glazed in July 1938 and at the same time doors were fitted on this deck so that she could tender the Holland, America liner *Nieuw Amsterdam*. (*Targett*)

This photograph of 1900 shows the Bealing nurseries to be committed to supplying the needs of liners. (*Bealing/M10426*)

The Bealing home and business headquarters in Church Road, Sholing. (*Bealing/BB89/884*)

Greenhouses were necessary for providing out of season blooms. (*Bealing/BB89/884*)

A Bealing floral arrangement on the *Majestic* in April 1933. (*Bealing/TH8/148/1*)

A floral arrangement on the *Olympic* in March 1933. (*Bealing/TH8/148/1*)

The tradition continued into the 1960s. (*Phillips*/M22306)

A diver has been examining the quay wall in 1880. Here his air is supplied by a pump on land and not in the boat. The first recorded diving operation was in connection with the salvage of the *Tartar* in 1843. (*SCC*/M2552)

Maintenance of navigation aids was originally the responsibility of the Harbour Commissioners, later the Harbour Board. The pioneering buoy designed by Captain Peacock in 1851 was remarkably similar to this one pictured in 1960. (*SCC/M8197*)

The Southampton Harbour Board launch *Triton* was an integral part of the groundbreaking Port Operation and Information Service, regulating not only the movement of ships but also of flying boats. (*Phillips/M16476*)

The Operations Room at Calshot Signal Station. Southampton was the first port in the world to adopt the principles of the International Maritime Conference in the Hague in 1957. The system was inaugurated by Rt Hon Harold Watkinson MP, Minister of Transport and Civil Aviation, on 17 January 1958. (*ABP*)

The sludge carrier *Shieldhall* was purchased by Southern Water from Strathclyde Regional Council in 1977, for the disposal of sewage at sea. A successful preservation group was set up in 1988 to maintain and operate her. (*SCC*)

The extensive fire of June 1906 also affected ships moored nearby. After the fire, the LSWR fire boat was kept in steam and capable of action which had not previously been the case.(*SCC/M4060*)

The Dock Fire Station which was lost during an air raid in World War Two and not replaced. (*SCC/M12265*)

Superintendent Melbourne Jones was in charge of the Dock Fire Station from 1923 to 1939. (SCC/M12268)

An Auxiliary Fire Service exercise in the Docks in 1939. (SCC/M11892)

Superintendent Jones and his crew with their Merryweather motor appliance. CR number plates were issued in Southampton between 1903 and 1925. (SCC/M12267)

Standard World War Two National Fire Service boat which, having been stationed in Southampton, was operated by Southampton Fire Brigade between 1948 and 1963. (*SCC/M11899*)

A fire on board the tug tender *Calshot*, being tackled *c*.1950. (*Phillips/M16623*)

Fireboat 39, built by Thornycroft and delivered to Southampton Fire Brigade in April 1963. This was their last boat. It passed to Hampshire Fire Brigade and was sold in 1987. (*Hants FRS/M11891*)

Ford delivery van of the Portswood Laundry from an advertisement of the 1920s. (*SCC/1670*)

Liners' Laundry Ltd., Freemantle, taking laundry bags for washing. (*Phillips/M16603*)

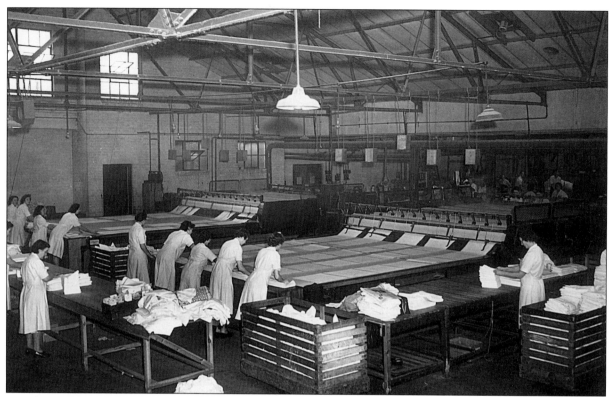

Laundry interior. It was a never-ending process, keeping big ships hygienic and habitable. Today large ships like the *QE2* have their own laundries. (*Phillips/M19112*)

The finished goods back on board. (*Phillips/M22406*)

A rare advertisement of about 1900 for the chandlery of Alderman Tilling. In today's international markets, this sort of business tends to be operated by firms with multiple outlets, such as Cosalt Perrys and Huttons of Hull. (*SCC*)

Seddon delivery van of Oakley & Watling, photographed when new in 1952. Eagle Warehouse of May & Baker the grocers, at the lower end of French Street, is a reminder of the number of specialist suppliers that once catered for the needs of ships. (*Phillips/M19007*)

Ice cream going on board *Queen Mary* by conveyor. Among other supplies required by ships is fresh water. The demands of the great liners like the Queens put a considerable strain on the local mains, and could even affect operations at the Philips semiconductor plant nearby. *(Phillips/M19248)*

The bonded warehouse of Hibbert's Brewery above Cadbury's distribution depot. Hibbert's, a company that supplied many of the leading shipping lines, also had bottling plant in the New Docks. The building, 'K' Warehouse, built in 1850, was sometimes known as 'Sugar House' from its original function. *(ABP/1582)*

A dredger off the Royal Pier in the 1890s, when maintaining the specified depth of water was the responsibility of the Harbour Commissioners. (*Borrough-Hill/93.1985*)

The James Dredging Co undertook such large-scale and continuous work in Southampton that they had their own boatyard in Northam. Tugs like *Foremost 108* were used to move equipment and to tow hopper barges. (*Phillips/M21008*)

Queen Mary appears to be hemmed in by this bucket dredger. Dredgers played an important part in the creation of the New Docks which was one of the world's largest civil engineering projects at the time. Construction of these docks is assumed to have started with James Dredging Co's dredger *Foremost III* commencing activity on 3 January 1927. (*Phillips/M16568*)

A later dredger *Foremost Southampton*, still of the bucket type. Associated British Ports have employed their own suction dredger *Swansea Bay* in recent years. (*SCC*)

Western Union commenced in Southampton in 1924. Their offices were staffed by uniformed messengers. From Southampton, a customer's message was sent by teleprinter to the company's London office where it was conveyed across the Atlantic by submarine cable. (*Phillips/M19240*)

Automobile Association Port Service dealing with imported vehicles *c.*1960, while, in the background, *Queen Elizabeth*'s paintwork is freshened up. (*SCC*)

Union Castle ship *Kenilworth Castle* being coaled laboriously in September 1935. (*Williamson/MM10162*)

A specialist banana carrier *Golfito* of Elders and Fyffes has the tank-cleaning vessel *Tulipfield* of British Wheeler Process Ltd alongside. (*Phillips/M16534*)

The Imperial Hotel was an independent venture adjacent to Southampton Terminus Station, but was taken over by the London and South Western Railway in 1870 and renamed the South Western Hotel. It remained as such until requisitioned by the Navy in 1940. The steam train is heading for the Royal Pier. (*SCC*)

Once the docks came into railway ownership, the LSWR operated its own docks police. This photograph of Constable (later Sergeant) James Holmes was taken in 1900. (*SCC/M11938*)

Today private security contractors are employed and Hampshire Constabulary operates this launch, *Earl Mountbatten of Burma*, to patrol the water. (*Picsales.com/6980-36A*)

Shipbuilding and Repair

THERE has been shipbuilding undertaken at Redbridge and at Bursledon since the 16th century. These were primarily warships, but coastal and fishing craft were built locally as need arose.

Since the arrival of the steamship and development of the docks, shipbuilding has been concentrated in a few hands. These firms have also undertaken repair work, and have all ventured into yacht building at some stage, Oswald, Mordaunt building one yacht, UNA in 1879.

On the west bank of the River Itchen the most famous enterprise was that ultimately known as Day Summers & Co at Northam Iron Works, The company had moved there from Foundry Lane, Millbrook in 1840, and built nearly 200 ships before they closed down in 1928.

Other ship building concerns located on this side of the river have been small in size and have included Joseph Hodgkinson, Cross House Engineering Works which operated from about 1850. This was later taken over by George Napier and Son, and turned out barges, tugs and small steamers, the 84ft steam-powered Thames barge *Record* of 1897 being a typical product.

Dibles (1918) Ltd was set up specifically to produce steel self-trimming colliers, the firm having produced wooden craft from 1840, and in 1920 the yacht builders Summers and Payne Ltd established a new steel ship building and repair yard at Millstone Point.

On the east bank of the River Itchen at Woolston, T.R. Oswald built his first ship in 1876. As Oswald, Mordaunt & Co this firm, noted for its large elegant sailing ships, continued until 1889. The site was then operated by Southampton Naval Iron Works between 1890 and 1893. Subsequently the yacht builders J.G. Fay and Mordey, Carney &

Co Ltd wishing to expand, jointly took over the site and operated it until selling to J.I. Thornycroft in 1904.

Thornycroft formed a ship repair department on the west bank in 1921 and in 1928, acquired the yard of Day Summers when that firm ceased trading, remaining there for many years. In 1966 Thornycroft amalgamated with the long-established Gosport firm of Vospers to form Vosper Thornycroft. In 1977, there followed a brief period of nationalisation of the shipbuilding industry and in 1998 there was further expansion in ship repair with the take over of Halmatic. The Halmatic yard had previously been operated by Hunting.

From the outset the Dock Company realised that ship repair was an integral part of their activities, and set out to provide dry docks for this purpose. Number 1 was opened in 1846. These were constructed to accommodate the largest ships then afloat. The dock owners have been in the habit of leasing their dry docks to other operators and No 4, which was the last dry dock constructed by the Southampton Dock Company, was used exclusively by the Union line for many years.

The docks then, have seen their share of ship repair work. All Oswald, Mordaunt ships came to the docks for fitting out. Day Summers could not accommodate HMS *Warrior* and so the work of converting her into an auxiliary workshop, HMS *Vernon*, was undertaken in the Outer Dock in June 1904. The same firm had won the contract to modify the *Great Eastern*, but she was so huge that the work was done where she was moored. This was in May 1860.

In February 1903, the London and South Western Railway completed the first vessel to be wholly built and launched in Southampton docks. This was the 85ft 6in steel fire float

Princess II. There are not known to have been any other launchings until construction of Mulberry Harbour components in 1944.

Ship repair facilities were greatly enhanced with the coming of Harland & Wolff when they established premises at Trafalgar Dry Dock (No 6). This firm had a close association with White Star Line, which had transferred some of its routes to Southampton in 1907. White Star now needed Harland's facilities to be available locally, although one of the first major jobs undertaken in this dry dock, the reconstruction of the *Suevic*, required the skills of J.I. Thornycroft.

Trafalgar Dry Dock was later used by Vosper ship repairers, and in April 1987 was taken over by Thew Marine, which took over the King George V Dry Dock (No 7) at the same time. Trafalgar dry dock was taken out of use in June 1989 while in 1990 A. & P. Southampton Ltd took over No 7, the last remaining dry dock.

Other ship repair facilities included the slipway of S. Spencer & Co which opened in 1957 and was sandwiched between Thornycroft's Woolston yard and the Regent Oil depot; and Husband's Shipyard at Marchwood which commenced ship repair in 1922. Husband's jetty was extend by 500ft in 1957 with the prospect of undertaking some tanker work. This famous yard closed in 1998.

Ship building elsewhere in Southampton has included the West Quay Boat Yard of John Peckett and Sons, builders of the Royal Mail tender UNA, and of course the products of the British Power Boat Co at Hythe.

While Southampton is not noted for ship breaking, the firm of Pollock Brown, operating from the old Day Summers yard on the Itchen, cut up some 32 small ships between 1948 and 1960. In later years, scrap metal became an important export, much of it going to Spain. European Metal Recycling Ltd now operates the yard and exports over 100,000 tonnes of scrap per year.

Oswald, Mordaunt's yard photographed from the Woolston side in about 1877 judging by the stage of development of the docks opposite. The ship yard, seen here while empty, comprises a fenced area and two wooden huts in the centre of the picture. (*Romsey/54/1231*)

By the time of the overhaul of the *Albuera* in about 1880, more substantial buildings have appeared. Although the products – both iron and wooden ships – were well built, the yard had a bad reputation regarding the safety of its workers. (*SCC*)

Vessels seem to have been built in a dock rather than on a slipway. The stern of *Albuera* under repair in Oswald Mordaunt's yard. She was built in Moulmein in 1854 and was lost in 1883. (*SCC*)

Brunel's steamship *Great Eastern* creating a lot of interest when moored off Netley Hospital. She was brought to Southampton after launching and modified by Day Summers in 1860. (*SCC*)

Three stages in the construction of the salvage ship *Safeguard* at Day Summers' Northam Ironworks in 1914. In the first picture, the keel has just been laid. (*SCC/M9538*)

The hull plating is almost complete. The ship was bult for T. Ensor, London. (*SCC/M9537*)

Safeguard is going to have a wooden deck, but there is some riveting still going on in the background. *SCC/M6539)*

Boom defence vessel *BD23*, built by Day Summers *c.*1916, after fitting out. Four of these vessels were built by the firm. *(SCC)*

Admiralty rescue tug *Ocean Eagle* during World War One. She was originally built by Day Summers as the *St Athan*. (*SCC*)

Party assembled for the launch of the coaster *Allanwater* from Day Summers' yard, with the workers who built her looking on in the foreground. The launch date was 14 October 1920. (*SCC/M9529B*)

Day Summers machine shop in 1921. The central area is flanked by several large lathes with the floor in the middle of the building being used as an erecting area, in this case for a marine steam engine. Day Summers also produced machinery not for marine use, or for ships other than their own. (*SCC/M6013*)

The outer extremities of the machine shop are packed with smaller machine tools. (*SCC/M15544*)

Cynthia Szlumper, the daughter of the Dock and Marine manager launches the new Southern Railway paddle steamer *Shanklin* at the Thornycroft yard on 6 June 1924. (*Szlumper/M10288*)

Canadian destroyer *Saguenay* launched from the Thornycroft yard in July 1930. (*Kennaway/1B10*)

Interior of Thornycroft's Turbine Shop in 1935 showing the open turbine casings for HMS *Grafton* and HMS *Glowworm*. The rotors are in the background. These were the two main craft built that year. (*SCC*)

HMS *Magpie* undergoing trials before her handover by Thornycroft to the Royal Navy in 1935. (*SCC/M9613*)

A rather desolate view of the Thornycroft yard photographed in February 1938 from the deck of the vessel *Mohawk*. (*Thornycroft*)

The scene at Woolston as recorded by the dock photographer in November 1942. (*ABP*)

Construction of Floating Bridge No 12 in 1964, one of the last floating bridges for use on the Itchen. It is in an advanced stage of construction on the slipway at Thornycroft's, and was launched on 11 June. (*Thornycroft/6429*)

Menzel Bourquiba, one of a pair of patrol boats for the Tunisian Navy, designed and built by Vosper Thornycroft. She is seen on her trials in November 1977. (*Vosper Thornycroft/M12010*)

The Vosper Thornycroft ship yard with covered slipways. Not only do these protect the ship and the workers from the elements, they are essential when moulding large hulls in glass-reinforced plastic. (*Vosper Thornycroft/17733*)

A row of first-generation service tenders under construction at Hythe in 1931. They display the characteristic shape of the products of the British Power Boat Company during this period. (*Scott-Paine/M14398.3*)

Early Day Summers patent 'steam sheers' were set up for repair work at the entrance to the Outer Dock in about 1850. These were a sort of heavy lift crane which, although unable to turn, could bring a load to land by movement of the back stay. (*ABP/1590*)

DAY, SUMMERS & CO., Limited,

ENGINEERS, BOILERMAKERS, SHIP & YACHT BUILDERS, Northam Iron Works, SOUTHAMPTON.

CONTRACTORS TO THE

Admiralty,
War Office,
Russian
    Government,
Spanish
    Government,
Egyptian
    Government,
Argentine
    Government.

25-Ton FLOATING SHEERS.

85 Sets of these Sheers have now been made by D. S. & CO., Ltd.

Specialities: STEAM TRIPOD TRAVERSING SHEERS (Land and Floating), and HAULING-UP SLIP MACHINERY.

Advertisement for Day Summers sheer legs which were exported to many parts of the world. The advertisement also mentions their non-fleeting slipway machinery for hauling ships of up to 1,000 tons out of the water. This was patented in 1864 and again was widely used. (*SCC*)

The hydraulic machinery for operating the lock gates to the Inner Dock was produced by what was then known as Summers and Day, and is dated 1855. It is seen here in use 95 years later. (*ABP/2408/1*)

The Prince of Wales, later Edward VIII, opened the floating dry dock by sailing through the submerged structure in the paddle steamer *Duchess of Fife* on 12 July 1924. Subsequently the Union Castle liner *Arundel Castle*, demonstrated the working of the dock. (*Bell*)

The impact of the floating dry dock on the town can be seen in this Hoffmann postcard. When built by Vickers Armstrong, it was the largest floating dry dock in the world and was designed on a modular principle so that it could be extended by the insertion of new sections if necessary. Initially ordered by the London and South Western Railway, its delivery was delayed because of a strike by shipyard workers. (*Hoffmann/TH3-4/7*)

The floating dry dock was required in order that the White Star liner *Majestic*, then the largest liner in the world, could be maintained in Europe. Having become redundant with the building of the King George V Graving Dock, the floating dry dock went to Portsmouth in 1940. (*SCC*)

Dry Dock No 3 in July 1935 with three yachts, *Candida*, *Yankee* and, in the foreground, *Britannia*. While the original group of dry docks was becoming too small for commercial shipping, this was the age of giant yachts. (*Bealing/M9662*)

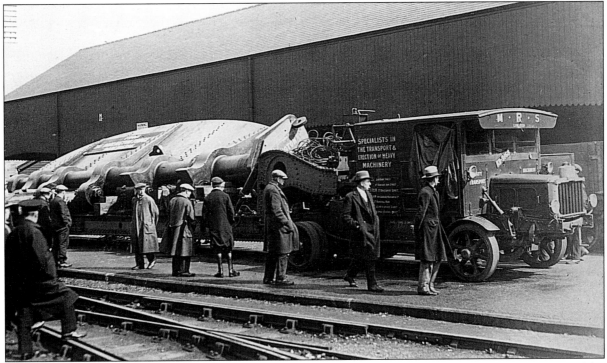

The rudder of the Cunard liner *Berengaria* arrives from Darlington Forge Co in the vicinity of Trafalgar Dry Dock in April 1932 after having been sent by road for repairs. The journey added two weeks to the job. (*Bealing/M9623*)

Dry Dock No 4
with two 'J' Class
yachts, *Shamrock
V* and *Astra*,
photographed in
1931. *Shamrock V*
was the last yacht
used by Sir
Thomas Lipton in
his attempt to win
the Americas Cup.
(*Bealing*/M9664)

Opening of the King George V Graving Dock, then the largest dry dock in the world, by King George V. He arrived on 26 July 1933 on board the Royal Yacht *Victoria and Albert*. (*SCC/299.1987*)

An engineering works was set up by Parsons for the overhaul of marine diesel engines adjacent to the Harland & Wolff works at Trafalgar Dry Dock. It is seen here shortly after being built by the local firm of Udall. (*Phillips/M20642*)

Collision damage to the coaster *Tarbek* of Hamburg. (*Phillips/M17238*)

Bransfield and *John Biscoe* at Vosper Thornycroft's Northam repair yard for their seasonal overhaul, in June 1975. (*Vosper Thornycroft/M11788*)

One of the steam Floating Bridges in for repair at Thornycrofts. The steam engines from two Day Summers-built floating bridges, Nos 8 and 10, were acquired in 2001 by the City Council with assistance from the Science Museum. As well as being of local interest, they illustrate archaic forms of marine steam engine. (*Vosper Thornycroft/5924*)

P & O *Arcadia* in King George V dry dock in March 1976. She was broken up three years later. (*Vosper Thornycroft/M11907.2*)

Trinity House light ship No 95 among the varied craft at Northam awaiting repair. Vosper Thornycroft fitted helicopter landing platforms to lightships towards the end of their lives and Camper & Nicholson, the yacht builders, also renovated light ships before closure of the Southampton works in 1979. (*Vosper Thornycroft/M11836*)

Trafalgar Dry Dock and the former ship repair facilities of Harland & Wolff, operated by Vosper Thornycroft when this photograph was taken in October 1976. The former BOAC flying boat terminal in the foreground became HMS *Wessex*, the home of the Solent Division of the RNVR in June 1957, and has their 'ton' class coastal minesweeper HMS *Warsash* moored alongside. (*Vosper Thornycroft/7024*)

Herald Of Free Enterprise in Trafalgar Dry Dock for repair by Vosper Thornycroft in September 1980. She was not used in Southampton but is a reminder of the Thoresen 'drive-through' principle on which modern ferries depend. On 6 March 1987, she set sail from the Belgian port of Zeebrugge with her bow doors still open, and capsized. Of the 533 passengers on board the 8,000-tonne ship, 193 died. (*Vosper Thornycroft*/M11759)

Looking extremely forlorn, the paddle steamer *Balmoral* awaits her fate in the shipbreakers Pollock Brown. She had been requisitioned during both world wars and was worn out. *Balmoral* was the fourth ship to be broken by this firm after World War Two, a job that took from December 1948 to March 1949. (*Phillips/M21042*)

A later view of the Pollock Brown yard, which was originally part of the Day Summers works, showing the breaking of the yacht *Endeavour II* between October 1957 and February 1958. Shipbreaking at the yard ended in 1960. (*Phillips/M16583*)

Index